ONE NATION
UNDER GOD

One Nation Under God recounts the history of Christianity in the United States and looks at what may happen to America if she abandons her Christian foundations. The Founding Fathers based our government on Biblical principles—a fact affirmed by John Adams when he reminded Thomas Jefferson that "The general principles on which the fathers achieved independence were the general principles of Christianity. I will avow that I then believed, and now believe, that those general principles of Christianity are as eternal and immutable as the existence and attributes of God." Regrettably, many Americans have forgotten (or never heard of) those early foundations and consequently are allowing forces to move America away from many of the Biblical precepts that originally made her great. President Ronald Reagan wisely reminded Americans, "If we forget what we did, we won't know who we are ... [A]n eradication of the American memory could result, ultimately, in an erosion of the American spirit." *One Nation Under God* helps us remember who we are and what we did and thus helps preserve the American spirit.

David Barton, Historian, Author, and founder of *Wallbuilders*

It is my great pleasure to recommend to anyone who is interested in the truth of our Christian American heritage, the book, *One Nation under God,* by Leon G. Stevens.

It is refreshing to see an accurate account of our founding fathers' desires to build a nation that rested on Christ's principles. Mr. Stevens actually quotes many of our nations great leaders from the past.

This book will stir the heart of anyone who reads it to be a voice for Christ in our nation.

Dr. David Teis, Founder and Senior Pastor of
Liberty Baptist Church in Las Vegas

Leon Stevens has carefully researched and written an excellent history of America's religious heritage. He has given us a book that everyone should read who is concerned about how our religious heritage is seemingly being rewritten by some who want to minimize or take God out of our nation's history. This book should be in every person's library who wants to know from the actual words and writings of our forefathers, what our incredible history truly is. I recommend this book for every Christian who cares about our beloved America!

Dr. David Gibbs, Author, Evangelist and founder of Christian Law Association.

"I have reviewed the book *One Nation Under God* by Leon G. Stevens. I was delighted to see the overview study of early Americans and their Christian faith. In this day of "revisionist history" we must do all we can to place into print and into the hands of American citizens the nature of our Christian heritage. I am thankful to have this resource available."

Dr. Paul Chappell, Author, Pastor Lancaster Baptist Church, Founder West Coast Baptist College

If my people, which are called by my name, shall humble themselves, and pray, and seek my face, and turn from their wicked ways; then will I hear from heaven, and will forgive their sin, and will heal their land.

2 Chronicles 7:14 (KJV)

1Judge me, O God, and plead my cause against an ungodly nation: O Deliver me from the deceitful and unjust man. 2For thou art the God of my strength: why dost thou cast me off? Why go I mourning because of the oppression of the enemy? 3O send out thy light and thy truth: let them lead me; let them bring me unto thy holy hill, and to thy tabernacles. 4Then will I go unto the altar of God, unto God my exceeding joy: yea, upon the harp will I praise thee, O God my God. 5Why art thou cast down, O my soul? And why art thou disquieted within me? Hope in God: for I shall yet praise him, who is the health of my countenance, and my God.

Psalm 43:1-5 (KJV)

ONE NATION UNDER GOD

*A Factual History of
America's Religious Heritage*

LEON G. STEVENS

NEW YORK

ONE NATION UNDER GOD

A Factual History of America's Religious Heritage

ISBN 978-1-61448-809-5 paperback
ISBN 978-1-61448-810-1 hard cover
ISBN 978-1-61448-812-5 eBook
Library of Congress Control Number: 2013945995

Morgan James Publishing
The Entrepreneurial Publisher
5 Penn Plaza, 23rd Floor,
New York City, New York 10001
(212) 655-5470 office • (516) 908-4496 fax
www.MorganJamesPublishing.com

Cover Design by:
Rachel Lopez
www.r2cdesign.com

Interior Design by:
Bonnie Bushman
bonnie@caboodlegraphics.com

In an effort to support local communities, raise awareness and funds, Morgan James Publishing donates a percentage of all book sales for the life of each book to Habitat for Humanity Peninsula and Greater Williamsburg.

Get involved today, visit
www.MorganJamesBuilds.com.

Habitat for Humanity®
Peninsula and
Greater Williamsburg
Building Partner

DEDICATION

This book is dedicated to the two people that have most influenced my Christian life and have been an inspiration in the creation of this book.

Joshua David Teis, Pastor of Southern Hills Baptist Church, Las Vegas, Nevada and Don McNiel, the brother I always wanted and never had.

Pastor Teis has been a mentor and spiritual leader in my life. He has helped me grow as a Christian and has encouraged me throughout the writing of this book. He has been a true and loving friend.

Don McNiel has been my anchor on my path to salvation. He has been a confidant and inspiration in my walk with God. Don spent many hours in helping me to find the right Scriptural passages to use throughout this work.

Without the influence of these two men I don't think I could have created this work dedicated to the salvation of our great nation.

TABLE OF CONTENTS

Dedication   xi

Preface   xv

Acknowledgments   xvii

Chapter One: The Founding of a Christian Nation   1

    The First "Great Awakening"   2

    From Enlightenment To A New Nation   11

    The Revolutionary War   14

    The Founding Fathers   27

    The Second "Great Awakening"   68

    Strength for a Christian Nation   72

    The Civil War   81

Chapter Two: Leading a Christian Nation   87

Chapter Three: Educating a Christian Nation   121

Chapter Four: The Decline of a Christian Nation   133

Chapter Five: Outlawing Religious Education in a Christian Nation   161

Chapter Six: Taking Back Our Christian Nation   173

Endnotes   185

PREFACE

Some people think we Americans are the new Israelites. The parallel being the Israelites were in Egypt for 400 years to learn the truth about God. The Puritans came to America almost 400 years ago to be able to have the freedom to learn the truth about God. After being released from bondage in Egypt, the Israelites praised God and then turned away from Him. Just as we, as a nation, are turning away from Him now.

The Puritans and Pilgrims came to the New World to escape religious persecution in Europe to found a land that they thought could be the new Garden of Eden, and they would build a "new Jerusalem." Their legacy was one of religious freedom for all.

Our Founding Fathers sought to keep that legacy alive when they started this grand experiment called The United States of America. It would be a nation built on the same foundation as that of the Puritans, **"One Nation Under God."**

I have a passion for the history of America and its founding. I am a Christian and a patriot and am very concerned about the direction our country is heading. This nation was founded on Judeo-Christian principles as evidenced by the writings and letters of our Founding Fathers.

For the past forty-five years our country has taken away the very foundation upon which our country was built. When I heard our national leaders state "we are not a Christian nation," I was determined to set the story straight.

ACKNOWLEDGMENTS

I would like to thank my wife Sandie for the countless hours she spent proof reading my work and giving me the encouragement and love that help create this historical account.

My gratitude goes out to Ira M. Bowman for creating the original cover design for *One Nation Under God*. He also spent many hours formatting the illustrations and pictures in this book.

Thank you so much to the many members of Southern Hills Baptist Church of Las Vegas, Nevada who have supported me both morally and financially. Without their prayers and encouragement I may not have completed this work.

My heart felt thanks and gratitude go to my editors; Fred W. Murray, Kayla Tillman, Darlene Dahl, and Denise Miller for the many countless hours spent in editing my work. If not for the leadership of Fred W. Murray, Administrative Pastor of Southern Hills Baptist Church in Las Vegas, Nevada, the work never would have been reviewed, edited and prepared for the republishing of "One Nation Under God" to reach a larger audience. God bless them all.

I must also acknowledge the blessings from our Father in Heaven for giving me the desire to begin writing this book and the strength to finish it.

THE FOUNDING OF A
CHRISTIAN NATION

Before we can bring our nation back to the Glory of God we must first understand how and why our country was created for the Glory of God.

We have been hearing from our political leaders that we are not a Christian nation. It seems we are heading that way. Our children can't pray in school, displaying the Ten Commandments in a courthouse is being challenged and we can't even have the Cross displayed on government land! The list goes on and on. Some people in this country want to forbid displaying the name of God or practicing his teachings in public.

Just as Peter and the other disciples were forbidden from preaching in the name of Jesus by their religious leaders, we too are being forbidden from honoring Jesus in public by our government and some atheist groups.

We must be like the apostles and pray, worship, and honor God no matter what the government says. We must change our government so we can truly be like the apostles.

Then the captain went with the officers, and brought them without violence, for they feared the people, lest they should be stoned. And when they had brought them, they set them before the council: and the high priest asked them, Saying, Did not we straitly command you that ye should not teach in this name? and, behold, ye have filled Jerusalem with your doctrine...Then Peter and the other apostles answered and said: "We ought to obey God rather than men....

Acts 5:26-32 (KJV)

When Israel turned away from God, He delivered them to the Philistines. Then the Philistines captured the Ark of the Covenant, which was for the Glory of God. **1 Samuel 4:21 says** *"...The glory has departed from Israel".* This could we be true of our nation, if like Israel, we continue to turn our back on God.

There has been a lot written in recent years to try to dismiss the fact that America was founded upon Judeo-Christian principles and ethics. Anyone who examines the original writings of our Founding Fathers will find an abundance of quotations showing the profound extent to which Christianity influenced their thinking and lives.

Between 1629 and 1640 the Puritans moved to the New World in order to establish a country where they were free to worship as they chose. Puritans were members of a number of religious groups advocating more "purity" of worship and doctrine. In other words, they believed in truth from the Bible, not the pulpit.

The colonies were established precisely to serve as religious sanctuaries for various denominations of the Christian church; Pennsylvania, a Quaker state; Maryland, a Catholic state; and Massachusetts, a Puritan state.

THE FIRST "GREAT AWAKENING"

During the late seventeen and early eighteenth century, Colonial America saw some major changes. American cities became important seaports and the southern part of America was becoming a major contributor to the Colonial American's economy. In addition, the population was increasing with immigrants coming in large numbers due to the growth of plantations. As a result of this economic and population boom people were beginning to question the role of government with regard to religion and human nature. This brought about a major religious revival to Colonial America. Referred to as "The Great Awakening and Enlightenment" it revived interests in education, science and literature. "The Enlightenment" also challenged the role of religion and divine right. This helped Colonial America to see that it was possible to challenge the king and his divine right.

The movement fulfilled people's need for reassurance, direction and religious purpose, which was otherwise missing. People united in the understanding of the Christian faith and life. The movements also led to creation of different sects and denominations, and advocated religious tolerance. This movement saw traditional authority of the clergy being challenged and their success made it easier to challenge the authority of the King.

Jonathan Edwards (1703–1758)

In 1726, Edwards succeeded his grandfather, Solomon Stoddard, as the pastor of the church in Northampton, Massachusetts, the largest and most influential church outside of Boston.

From 1734 to 1735, Edwards oversaw some of the initial stirrings of the First Great Awakening. He gained international fame as a revivalist and "theologian of the heart" after publishing A Faithful Narrative of the Surprising Work of God (1738), which described the awakening in his church and served as an empirical model for American and British revivalists alike.

The widespread revivals of the 1730s and 1740s stimulated one of the two most fruitful periods for Edwards's writings. In this period, Edwards became very well known as a revivalist preacher who subscribed to an experiential interpretation of Reformed theology that emphasized the sovereignty of God, the depravity of humankind, the reality of hell, and the necessity of a "New Birth" conversion. While critics assailed the convictions of many supposed converts as illusory and even the work of the devil, Edwards became a brilliant apologist for the revivals. In *The Distinguishing Marks of a Work of the Spirit of God* (1741), *Some Thoughts Concerning the Present Revival* (1742), *A Treatise Concerning Religious Affections* (1746), and *The Life of David Brainerd* (1749), he sought to isolate the signs of true sainthood from false belief.[1]

Jonathan Edwards was considered by many to be the greatest theologian America produced. When he began preaching in Northampton, Massachusetts in 1734, the moral conditions were at an extreme low, as was prevalent throughout most of the American colonies. Under his preaching that stressed the importance of an immediate personal spiritual rebirth, a revival began in his church among the youth and then spread to the adults. Edwards wrote that:

> In the spring and summer following, anno 1735, the town seemed to be so full of the presence of God; it never was so full of love nor of joy, and yet so full of distress, as it was then.

In two years, three hundred converts were added to the church, and the news of the revival spread throughout New England.

Edwards' writings are pondered and evaluated to the present day. His famous sermon "Sinners in the Hands of an Angry God" is still being read and studied in America's public schools as a specimen of eighteenth-century literature. Students of American history pay much attention to Edwards's scientific, philosophical, and psychological writings; theologians and church historians regard Edwards's work on revivals as unexcelled in analysis and scope. Christians continue to read his sermons with great appreciation for their rich doctrine, clear and forceful style, and powerful depiction of the majesty of God, the sinfulness of sin, and Christ's power to save.

For us to see Jonathan Edwards ascend his pulpit today, a candle in one hand and his sermon manuscript in the other, would cause a titter in the congregation. From our modern foam-cushioned church seats, with carpeted aisles and soothing background music, we can scarcely capture the old-time dignity of the unpretentious church where Edwards and others held captive the hearts and minds of their hearers.

When Jonathan Edwards "uttered" in the Spirit, the expressionless face, the sonorous voice and the sober clothing were forgotten. He was neither a dullard nor a sluggard. His was a devoted heart intent on rightly dividing the word of truth. But in doing it, Edwards flamed. Yet to him, sensationalism was an abomination. To make an impression was never the thought behind any of his preaching. Scholarship on fire for God is what Edwards had.

The tongue of Edwards must have been like a sharp two-edged sword to his attentive hearers. His words must have been as painful to their hearts and consciences as burning metal on flesh. Nevertheless, men gave heed, repented, and were saved.

"Knowing the terror of the Lord" (a thing seemingly forgotten in our day both by pulpit and pew), Edwards smoldered with holy wrath. Impervious to any consequences of such severity, he thundered these words from his pulpit:

> The bow of God's wrath is bent, and His arrows made ready upon the string. Justice points the arrow at your heart and strings the bow. It is nothing but the mere pleasure of God (and that of an angry God without any promise or obligation at all) that keeps the arrow one moment from being made drunk with your blood.

To utter truth like that with tears and tenderness takes an anointed and therefore fearless and compassionate man.

In the hearts and minds of the hearers there must also have been some prevenient grace at work. Apart from this, men would have rebelled at this stern sweep of power on their souls. As it was, before Edwards' spiritual hurricane, the crowd collapsed. Some fell to the earth as if pole-axed. Others, with heads bowed, clung onto the posts of the temple as if they were afraid of falling into the nethermost depths of hell.[2]

> *Behold, the day of the LORD cometh, cruel both with wrath and fierce anger, to lay the land desolate: and he shall destroy the sinners thereof out of it.*
>
> **–Isaiah 13:9 (KJV)**

George Whitefield (1714–1770)

America's "Great Awakening" was really started by George Whitefield mostly due to his 1739–1740 preaching tour. Whitefield made seven separate trips in nine years preaching all across the colonies. Little known today, Whitefield was America's first celebrity. According to historical documents, about 80 percent of all American's heard him preach at least once. When George Whitefield was in the area, farmers and shopkeepers alike would stop  what they were doing and go to the field where he was preaching. Every where he went, Whitefield was followed with people clamoring to hear him preach.

Whitefield pioneered most methods used in the 1700s evangelical revivals, including preaching in fields instead of churches. His farewell sermon on Boston Common drew 23,000 people (more than the entire population of Boston). In one week he would often preach a dozen or more times and spend forty to fifty hours in the pulpit. He was an orator without equal in the pulpit. His delivery was not the classical oratory with finely ornamented style, soaring flights of fancy and elegance of taste. His preaching was marked by biblical content, doctrinal emphasis and rhetorical simplicity. His delivery, however, was dramatic.

George Whitefield became a close friend of Benjamin Franklin who once estimated that Whitefield could be heard by thirty thousand people without amplification.

Whitefield pushed himself so hard and preached with such intensity that often afterward he had "a vast discharge from the stomach, usually with a considerable quantity of blood."[3]

In the fall of 1770, Whitefield was on an exhausting New England preaching tour, preaching in Boston, Portsmouth, and Exeter. When he reached Newbury Port, he was too tired to get out of the boat. With help, he made it to the parsonage of Old South Church. As evening came he regained a measure of strength and took supper with his host family. A crowd began to gather at the door. Some of them pushed on into the house in hope of hearing his voice again.

"I am too tired," Whitefield said "and must go to bed." He took a lighted candle and started climbing the stairs. But the sight of the patient people crowding into the hall and the street was too much to refuse. He paused on the staircase to say a few words. Soon he was preaching or "exhorting" as he called these impromptu addresses. As he urged them to trust the savior, he grew stronger, then weaker, then stronger again. He preached until the candle burned down to the socket and flickered out. Then one of the greatest of all preachers and evangelists went up to bed and died.[4]

In his lifetime, Whitefield preached at least eighteen thousand times. He addressed perhaps ten million people wanting to hear the Gospel and come to know Jesus Christ.

And the LORD commanded me at that time to teach you statutes and judgments, that ye might do them in the land whither ye go over to possess it.

–Deuteronomy 4:14 (KJV)

John Locke (1632–1704)

John Locke was considered the father of "liberalism" (belief in the importance of liberty and equality) and was regarded as one of the most influential of "Enlightenment" thinkers. His contributions to classical republicanism are reflected in our Declaration of Independence. In his most famous work, his "Two Treatises of Government" Locke set forth the belief that a successful government could be built only upon the transcendent, unchanging principles of natural law that were a subset of God's law. For example, he declared:

> The Law of Nature stands as an eternal rule to all men, legislators as well as others. The rules that they make for other men's actions must ... be conformable to the Law of Nature, i.e., to the will of God.
>
> Laws human must be made according to the general laws of Nature, and without contradiction to any positive law of Scripture, otherwise they are ill made. [5]

Locke's *Two Treatises of Government* were heavily relied upon the Founding Fathers. In fact, signer of the Declaration, Richard Henry Lee, declared that the Declaration itself was "copied from Locke's *Treatise on Government.*" Yet so heavily did Locke draw from the Bible in developing his political theories that in his first treatise on government, he invoked the Bible in one thousand three hundred forty nine references; in his second treatise, he cited it one hundred fifty seven times.

The Great Awakening and its impact

The Great Awakening grew out of the sense that religion was becoming an increasingly unimportant part of people's lives. In practical terms, this may well have been true. In Virginia, the most populous colony, the supply of ministers compared to the potential number of congregants was small, and churches in the backcountry were rare. The religious revival's leading figures were Congregationalist minister Jonathan Edwards and English evangelist George Whitefield, both dynamic preachers. Edwards was renowned for his "fire and brimstone" sermons that warned sinners about the fate God had in store for them if they did not repent. On numerous trips to the colonies beginning in 1738, Whitefield brought his message about the need for each individual to experience a "new birth" on the path to personal salvation (what today's fundamentalist Christians call being "born again").

The Great Awakening took on the proportions of a mass movement. Tens of thousands of people came to hear Whitefield preach as he moved from town to town, often holding meetings in the open or under tents, and he became a household name throughout the colonies. Moreover, the Great Awakening appealed to the heart, not the head. One of the reasons for its success was the emotion and drama that the revivalists brought to religion. The highlight of many of the services was the ecstatic personal testimony of those who had experienced a "new birth."

There is little doubt that the Great Awakening contributed to an increase in church membership and the creation of new churches. Slaves and Indians converted to Christianity in significant numbers for the first time, and the more evangelical sects, such as the Baptist and Methodist, grew. A rough estimate puts the number of religious organizations in the colonies in 1775 at more than three thousand. At the same time, the Great Awakening promoted religious pluralism. As the road to salvation was opened to everyone through personal conversion, doctrinal differences among the Protestant denominations became less important.

The religious movement is also often credited with encouraging the creation of new institutions of higher learning. Princeton University, founded as the College of New Jersey in 1746, grew out of the early revivalist William Tennent's Log College. Others established during the Great Awakening include Columbia University (King's College, 1754, Anglican), Brown University (Rhode Island College, 1764, Baptist), Rutgers (Queens College, 1766, Dutch Reformed), and Dartmouth College (1769, Congregationalist).[5]

Overall, religion was an important part of the colonization of America. It became a dominate part of the lives of the colonists and continued to grow over the years. Events such as the Salem Witchcraft Trials of the 1690s and the Great Awakening of the 1730s only increased the influence of religion in America. America had become a refuge for those who wanted religious freedom and become a home to the many people that had the chance to improve their lives.

Because the First Great Awakening served to build up interests that were Colonial in character had increased opposition to the Anglican Church (The Church of England) and the royal officials who supported it, many historians say it helped set in motion a democratic spirit that eventually brought America its political freedoms.[6]

The Revival period of our history also showed the need to teach the Gospel to our children so they would have a good Christian foundation to grow in life.

And ye shall teach them your children, speaking of them when thou sittest in thine house, and when thou walkest by the way, when thou liest down, and when thou risest up.

–Deuteronomy 11:19 (KJV)

Enlightenment brings Revolution

The American Revolution and many of the events to follow, was a culmination of many of the ideas of the Enlightenment. The Revolution came about after a series of unfair taxes upon the colonists by the British government, who needed this extra income to help them recover from their wars abroad. Until this point, the colonists were only paying taxes that would go to support localized projects and these taxes, most notably the Stamp Tax and the taxes on tea, were seen as completely unwarranted. Using the Enlightenment principles of freedom and reason, the colonists declared these taxes unfair and stood up against oppression. These early Americans wished to have their own government that was based on Enlightenment principles and thus the Revolution occurred. Locke's conception of natural rights for all of mankind was being violated by British oppression and it became necessary to draft a government and code that was conducive to guaranteeing everyone natural rights under law.

One of the first steps in the formation of the United States that was based upon Enlightenment ideals, was the creation of the Declaration of Independence. This sought to promise personal freedom to all citizens and this was to be guaranteed by means of a new form of government, one that was based on the people's right to have a say in their government. As the country moved toward the drafting of the Constitution, the ideas of several Enlightenment philosophers shaped the direction American political leaders took.

Another way that the Enlightenment helped to shape the colonies was in terms of religion. With the Great Awakening came a new understanding of America's early relationship to God and the Church. Instead of one all-powerful church that almost required membership, Protestant ideals based on Enlightenment principles of free will and freedom from institutions, allowed people to choose membership in a church rather than be forced into one. Although during the Enlightenment era there was a very secular focus in Europe, in America this was not the case. The colonies were still very religious, but they used the idea of their freedom to choose based on the Enlightenment principles. Instead of being tied to one religious authority, there were many choices in the colonies and people had a right to choose how to establish and maintain their connection to God.

Key figures in the founding of the United States such, as Thomas Jefferson, were greatly influenced by the ideas of the Enlightenment, which meant that the country was as well. Jefferson was a perfect man of the Enlightenment, as he was classically educated and trained in the humanities, as well as very practical and empirical. As the author of the Declaration of Independence, Jefferson shaped the country by solidifying the ideas of natural rights in terms of government and religion.

At this time, the Church of England (also known as the Anglican Church) was the established religion of Virginia. This meant that the Anglican Church was the only officially recognized church in the colony. Virginia taxpayers supported this church through a religion tax. Only Anglican clergymen could lawfully conduct marriages. Non-Anglicans had to get permission (a license) from the Colonial government to preach.

Shortly before the outbreak of the Revolutionary War, an evangelical Baptist preacher named "Swearing Jack" Waller attempted to lead a prayer meeting without a license from the Colonial government of Virginia. Because he was violating Virginia's religion laws, "Swearing Jack" was jerked off his platform by sheriff's men who proceeded to beat his head against the ground. The sheriff then lashed him twenty times with a horsewhip.

On the eve of the Revolutionary War, nine of the thirteen colonies supported official religions with public taxes. Moreover, in these colonies, the government dictated "correct" religious belief and methods of worship. Religious dissenters, like "Swearing Jack," were discriminated against, disqualified from holding public office, exiled, fined, jailed, beaten, mutilated, and sometimes even executed. Only Rhode Island, Pennsylvania, New Jersey, and Delaware did not have a system linking church and state. After the Revolution, leaders like Jefferson and Madison worked to ensure freedom of religion for all citizens of the new nation.

A year after Thomas Jefferson drafted the Declaration of Independence, he wrote a bill on religious freedom for his home state of Virginia. In writing these documents, Jefferson was strongly influenced by the 17th century English philosopher John Locke. In 1689, Locke had argued that "the church itself is a thing absolutely separate and distinct from the commonwealth [government]." Taking this idea from Locke, Jefferson proposed that Virginia end all tax support of religion and recognize the natural right of all persons to believe as they wish.[7]

Jefferson introduced his bill to the Virginia Assembly in 1779, but state lawmakers did not consider the matter of church and state until after the Revolutionary War.

Jefferson's Bill for "Establishing Religious Freedom" states:

> Almighty God hath created the mind free, and all attempts of influence it by temporal punishments or burdens, or by civil incapacitations, tend only to beget habits of hypocrisy and meanness, and are a departure from the plan of the Holy Author of our religion, who being Lord both of body and mind...." Jefferson wanted to extend the Gospel by "its influence on reason alone.

In addition, Thomas Jefferson understood the importance of education in making these ideals work in the new nation and founded the University of Virginia. In many ways, Jefferson represents the way Enlightenment ideals could be put into practice in the new colonies. Other men, such as Benjamin Franklin, were similar, since they had such a hand in formulating many of the institutions and tracts the country is based on, their Enlightenment ideas live on.

Without the Enlightenment as the philosophical basis of this country, one can only imagine how different life would be today. Important guarantees of human and natural rights, expressions of freedom and the rights of citizens to have free choice and practice religious freedom are all vital aspects in America still. Locke, Newton, and other Enlightenment thinkers put forth ideas about liberty and personal will that went on to be key aspects in the most important documents in America such as the Declaration of Independence and the Constitution.[8]

FROM ENLIGHTENMENT TO A NEW NATION

The Continental Congress, that governed the United States from 1774 to 1789, contained an extraordinary number of deeply religious men. The amount of energy that Congress invested in encouraging the practice of religion in the new nation exceeded that expended by any subsequent American national government. Although the Articles of Confederation did not officially authorize Congress to concern itself with religion, the citizenry did not object to such activities. This lack of objection suggests that both the legislators and the public considered it appropriate for the national government to promote a nondenominational, non-controversial Christianity.

Congress appointed chaplains for itself and the armed forces, sponsored the publication of a Bible, imposed Christian morality on the armed forces, and granted public lands to promote Christianity among the Indians. National days of thanksgiving and of "humiliation, fasting, and prayer" were proclaimed by Congress at least twice a year throughout the war. Congress was guided by "covenant theology," a Reformation doctrine especially dear to New England Puritans, which held that God bound himself in an agreement with a nation and its people. This agreement stipulated that they *should be prosperous or afflicted, according as their general Obedience or Disobedience thereto appears.* Wars and revolutions were, accordingly, considered afflictions, as divine punishments for sin, from which a nation could rescue itself by repentance and reformation.

The first national government of the United States was convinced that the "public prosperity" of a society depended on the vitality of its religion. Nothing less than a "spirit of universal reformation among all ranks and degrees of our citizens," Congress declared to the American people, would "make us holy, that so we may be a happy people."[9]

There was certainly no idea of separation of church and state in the minds of our Founding Fathers. Half of signers of the Declaration of Independence had some sort of divinity school training and twenty-nine of the fifty-six signers had seminary degrees. Are you aware that fifty-two of the fifty-six signers of The Declaration of Independence were orthodox, deeply committed Christians? The other three all believed in God, but had not declared a specific church. Even some of the supposed non-believers, such as Benjamin Franklin, found it necessary to turn to God in time of trouble. During the Constitutional Conventions most antagonistic moments, it was Franklin who not only offered a prayer but who added:

> Our prayers, Sir, were heard, and they were graciously answered. All of us who were engaged in the struggle must have observed frequent instances of the Superintending providence in our favor… And have we now forgotten that powerful friend? Or do we imagine that we no longer need His assistance?

Franklin not only went on to quote scripture, but also stated flatly that *"God governs the affairs of men."* That is not to say all of the Founding Fathers were Christians. But those who were not were deeply influenced by the principles of Christianity. The fact is, all of the Founding Fathers thought from a biblical perspective, whether they believed it or not.

The Declaration of Independence identified the source of all authority and rights as "Their Creator," and then emphasized that individual human rights were "God-given", not man made.

Samuel Adams said; "He who made all men hath made the truths necessary to human happiness obvious to all…Our forefathers opened the Bible to all".

Revolutionary War General, Henry Knox said: "…to the supreme head of the universe, to that great and tremendous Jehovah, Who created the universal frame of nature, worlds, and systems in number infinite…To this awfully sublime Being do I resign my spirit with unlimited confidence of His mercy and protection."

In 1792, the United State Congress approved a resolution that stated: "The congress of the United States recommends and approves the Holy Bible for use in all schools. They purchased and imported twenty thousand bibles to be made available to the American People."

In 1775, the Lutheran pastor John Peter Gabriel Muhlenberg preached a sermon on **Ecclesiastes 3:1**, *"To everything there is a season, a time for purpose under heaven."* Concluding the message, he declared, "In the language of the Holy Writ, there is a time for all things. There is a time to preach and a time to fight. And now is the time to fight." He then threw off his clerical robes to reveal the uniform of a Revolutionary Army officer.[10]

Ministers turned the revolution into a righteous cause and served at every level in the war, from military chaplains to taking up arms and leading troops into battle. The fact that ministers were so active in the military can only support the notion that we were founded on Christian principles and ethics. Why else would the ministers have put their reputations and their very lives on the line for the revolution?

After two main British armies were captured in 1777 and 1781, the other words of Patrick Henry proved true: "Three millions of people, armed with the *holy cause* of liberty, and in such a country as that which we possess, are invincible by any force which our enemy can send against us." (emphasis added).

THE REVOLUTIONARY WAR

Boston Tea Party

The passage of two major acts to collect more taxes angered the American colonists due to the intolerable imposition of these taxes without representation the of the colonies. The first was "The Stamp Act of 1765" which was an act for granting and applying certain stamp duties, and other duties, in the British colonies and plantations in America. The second was the passage of "The Townshend Act of 1767" was British legislation intended to raise revenue, tighten customs enforcement, and assert imperial authority in America. The key statute levied import duties on glass, lead, paint, paper, and tea. Its purpose was to provide salaries for some Colonial officials so that the provincial assemblies could not coerce them by withholding wages.

After years of these intolerable taxes and the curtailment of many liberties by the British and the deaths of five Americans killed at the hands of British soldiers in the Boston Massacre in March 1770, the men of Marlborough, Massachusetts in early 1773 unanimously declared:

> Death is more eligible than slavery. A free-born people are not required by the religion of Jesus Christ to submit to tyranny, but may make use of such power as God has given them to recover and support their laws and liberties...We implore the Ruler above the skies, that He would make bare His arm in defense of His Church and people, and let Israel go.

On December 16, 1773, the Sons of Liberty, a band of Boston patriots, threw 342 chests of tea from a British cargo ship into Boston Harbor. The British soon closed the Port of Boston and charged John Hancock, Samuel Adams, and others with "The Crime of High Treason". At the very least the "Boston Tea Party" rallied support in the thirteen colonies and sparked the Revolution.

> *The Lord has made bare His holy arm in the eyes of all the nations; and all the ends of the earth shall see the salvation of our God.*
> **–Isaiah 52:10 (KJV)**

Declaration of Independence

On July 2, 1776, the Continental Congress met in Philadelphia, Pennsylvania to declare independence from Great Britain.

The preamble and subsequent text of the Declaration of Independence does indeed refer to God and his guidance for the United States of America. It reads as follows:

> When, in the course of human events, it becomes necessary for one people to dissolve the political bonds which have connected them with another, and to assume among the powers of the earth, the separate and equal station to which the laws of nature and of nature's **_God_** entitle them, a decent respect to the opinions of mankind requires that they should declare the causes which impel them to the separation...We hold these truths to be self-evident, that all men are created equal, that they are endowed by their **_Creator_** with certain unalienable rights, that among these are life, liberty and the pursuit of happiness...We, therefore, the representatives of the United States of America, in General Congress, assembled, appealing to the **_Supreme Judge of the world_** for the rectitude of our intentions, do, in the name, and by the authority of the good people of these colonies, solemnly publish and declare, that these united colonies are, and of right ought to be free and independent states;... And for the support of this declaration, with a firm reliance on the **_protection of Divine Providence_**, we mutually pledge to each other our lives, our fortunes and our sacred honor. (emphasis added)

When George Washington gathered his troops on Long Island to prepare to meet the British to do battle in New York, he wrote in his general orders to his men that declared, as a nation, we serve under God. It reads in part:

> The time is now near at hand which must probably determine whether Americans are to be freemen or slaves... The fate of unborn millions will now depend, under God, on the courage and conduct of this army. Our cruel and unrelenting enemy leaves us no choice but a brave resistance, or the most abject submission; this is all we can expect....

...Let us therefore rely upon the goodness of the cause, and the aid of the supreme Being, in whose hands victory is, to animate and encourage us to great and noble actions. The eyes of all our countrymen are now upon us, and we shall have their blessing and praises....

Washington was a man of intense faith. As an elder in his church for almost twenty years, Washington always made God a priority. Many of those around him remarked on the sincerity of the first president's faith.

...for them that honour me I will honour, and they that despise me shall be lightly esteemed.

−1 Samuel 2:30 (KJV)

Proposed Seal for the United States

On July 4, 1776, Congress appointed Benjamin Franklin, Thomas Jefferson and John Adams "to bring in a device for a seal for the United States of America." Franklin's proposal adapted the biblical story of the parting of the Red Sea. Jefferson first recommended the "Children of Israel in the Wilderness, led by a Cloud by Day, and a Pillar of Fire by night..."

"Pharaoh sitting in an open Chariot, a Crown on his head and a Sword in his hand, passing through the divided Waters of the Red Sea in Pursuit of the Israelites: Rays from a Pillar of Fire in the Cloud, expressive of the divine Presence and Command, beaming on Moses who stands on the shore and extending his hand over the Sea causes it to overwhelm Pharaoh."

Motto: "Rebellion to Tyrants is Obedience to God"

Jefferson then embraced Franklin's proposal and rewrote it. The committee presented Jefferson's revision of Franklin's proposal to Congress on August 20.

Proposed Seal

Although not accepted these drafts reveal the religious temper of the Revolutionary period.[11]

The Reverend Jacob Duché first came to the attention of the First Continental Congress in September 1774, when he was summoned to Carpenters Hall to lead the opening prayers. Opening the session on the 7th of that month, he read the 35th Psalms, and then broke into a spontaneous prayer.

O Lord our Heavenly Father, high and mighty King of kings, and Lord of lords, who dost from thy throne behold all the dwellers on earth and reignest with power supreme and uncontrolled over all the Kingdoms, Empires and Governments; look down in mercy, we beseech thee, on these our American States, who have fled to thee from the rod of the oppressor and thrown themselves on Thy gracious protection, desiring to be henceforth dependent only on Thee, to Thee have they appealed for the righteousness of their cause; to Thee do they now look up for that countenance and support, which Thou alone canst give; take them, therefore, Heavenly Father, under Thy nurturing care; give them wisdom in Council and valor in the field; defeat the malicious designs of our cruel adversaries; convince them of the unrighteousness of their Cause and if they persist in their sanguinary purposes, of own unerring justice, sounding in their hearts, constrain them to drop the weapons of war from their unnerved bands in the day of battle! "Be Thou present, O God of wisdom, and direct the councils of this honorable assembly; enable them to settle things on the best and surest foundation. That the scene of blood may be speedily closed; that order, harmony and peace may be effectually restored, and truth and justice, religion and piety, prevail and flourish amongst The people. Preserve the health of their bodies and vigor of their minds; shower down on them and the millions they here represent, such temporal blessings as Thou seest expedient for them in this world and crown them with everlasting glory in the world to come. All this we ask In the name and through the merits of Jesus Christ, Thy Son and our Savior. Amen.

The opening session was not only to discuss the state of the nation; it was also a Bible study led by Reverend Duché.

Plead my cause, O Lord, with them that strive with me: fight against them that fight against me.

—Psalm 35:1

October 1, 1777, after Jacob Duché, Congress's first chaplain, defected to the British, Congress appointed joint chaplains: William White (1748-1836), Duché's successor at Christ Church, Philadelphia, and George Duffield (1732-1790), pastor of the Third Presbyterian Church of Philadelphia. By appointing chaplains of different denominations, Congress expressed a revolutionary social equality in religion and its desire to prevent any single denomination from monopolizing government patronage. The first Congress under the Constitution, which on April 15, 1789, adopted a joint resolution requiring that the practice be continued, followed this policy.

Continental Congress
National Thanksgiving Proclamations

Continental Congress issued the first ever National Thanksgiving Proclamation in 1777. It kept up the tradition of issuing Thanksgiving proclamations until 1784. In 1777, the United States Congress assembly set apart the 18th of December, which was a Thursday to be celebrated as the Thanksgiving Day and praise God. Next year, Congress designated the 30th of December, which was a Wednesday for public Thanksgiving and Praise Day, and it was announced that all people should express gratitude to Almighty with 'united hearts' so that he may grant favors upon the country of United States and bless with health and wealth.

Preparing for battle

It was the churches that became the primary source that stirred the fires of liberty, telling the colonists that the British government was usurping their God-given rights, and the king was violating the laws of God. The Founding Fathers were convinced that it was their sacred duty to start a revolution to uphold the law of God against the unjust and oppressive laws of men. The fight for political liberty was seen as a sacred cause because civil liberty was an inalienable right, according to God's natural law.

> *...we ought to obey God rather than men."*
>
> **–Acts 5:29 (KJV)**

One of the slogans of the American Revolution was "No king but King Jesus". For most of the patriots, their faith gave them the courage to believe in God's Word and risk their lives and properties to break the tyranny of British rule. In their Christian view, obedience to God took precedence over country or government. Their primary allegiance was to the Lord Jesus Christ.

Righteousness exalteth a nation...

—**Proverb 14:34 (KJV)**

Blessed is the nation whose God is the LORD...

—**Psalm 33:12 (KJV)**

Being armed with their faith in the Lord in one hand and the Bible in the other, the patriots of the American Revolution were set to do battle to create a new country to the Glory of God.

When thou goest out to battle against thine enemies, and seest horses, and chariots, and a people more than thou, be not afraid of them: for the Lord thy God is with thee, which brought thee up out of the land of Egypt.² And it shall be, when ye are come nigh unto the battle, that the priest shall approach and speak unto the people,³ And shall say unto them, Hear, O Israel, ye approach this day unto battle against your enemies: let not your hearts faint, fear not, and do not tremble, neither be ye terrified because of them;⁴ For the Lord your God is he that goeth with you, to fight for you against your enemies, to save you.

—**Deuteronomy 20:1–4 (KJV)**

Sink or Swim

William Prescott was the commander of the Colonial Militia at the Battle of Bunker Hill. In 1774, when the British blockaded the Boston Harbor, he wrote to the citizens of Boston:

We heartily sympathize with you, and are always ready to do all in our power for your support, comfort, and relief, knowing that Providence has placed you where you must stand the first shock. We consider that we are all embarked in the same boat and must sink or swim together... Let us all be of one heart, and stand fast in the liberty wherewith Christ has made us free. And may He, of His infinite mercy, grant us deliverance of all our troubles.[12]

Then I will give them one heart, and I will put a new spirit within them

—**Ezekiel 11:19 (KJV)**

Faith in God and the Bible were important to the revolutionary soldiers. So much so that the United States Congress authorized the printing of the first English language Bible to be printed in America. This was the only Bible printing ever called for by an act of Congress. It was "The 1782 Aitken Bible". Called "The Bible of the Revolution", it was small enough to fit into the coat pocket of the Revolutionary War soldiers. It measured only 6 inches tall by almost 4 inches wide. This King James Version of the Bible helped meet the need for scriptures while England refused to allow their Bibles to be imported by the colonists.

Articles of War

The Continental Congress debated for several days the Articles of War governing the conduct of the Continental Army. Altogether, these Rules and Regulations comprised sixty-nine separate articles. In the first twelve of the articles what kinds of behaviors were addressed and what kinds of punishments were to be meted out to violators. The Articles of War were finally established June 30, 1775. It was important to the Founding Fathers that the soldiers conducted themselves in a Godly manner, as evidenced by the following articles:

- Art. II. It is earnestly recommended to all officers and soldiers, diligently to attend Divine Service; and all officers and soldiers who shall behave indecently or irreverently at any place of Divine Worship, shall, if commissioned officers, be brought before a court-martial. There to be publicly and severely reprimanded by the President; if non-commissioned officers or soldiers, every person so offending, shall, for his first offence, forfeit One Sixth of a Dollar, to be deducted out of his next pay; for the second offence, he shall not only forfeit a like sum, but be confined for twenty-four hours, and for every like offence, shall suffer and pay in like manner; which money so forfeited, shall be applied to the use of the sick soldiers of the troop or company to which the offender belongs.

- Art. III. Whatsoever non-commissioned officer or soldier shall use any profane oath or execration, shall incur the penalties expressed in the second article; and if a commissioned officer be thus guilty of profane cursing or swearing, he shall forfeit and pay for each and every such offence, the sum of Four Shillings, lawful money.

- Art. IV. Any officer or soldier, who shall behave himself with contempt or disrespect towards the General or Generals, or Commanders in chief of the Continental Forces, or shall speak false words, tending to his or their hurt or dishonor, shall be punished according to the nature of his offence, by the judgment of a general court-martial.

Morality in the Navy

Congress particularly feared the navy as a source of moral corruption and demanded that skipper of American ships make their men behave. The first article in Rules and Regulations of the Navy, adopted on November 28, 1775, ordered all commanders to make sure that all sailors followed a moral code:

- Art. I. The Commanders of all ships and vessels belonging to the THIRTEEN UNITED COLONIES, are strictly required to shew in themselves a good example of honor and virtue to their officers and men, and to be very vigilant in inspecting the behaviour of all such as are under them, and to discountenance and suppress all dissolute, immoral and disorderly practices; and also, such as are contrary to the rules of discipline and obedience, and to correct those who are guilty of the same according to the usage of the sea.
- Art. II. The Commanders of the ships of the Thirteen United Colonies are to take care that divine service be performed twice a day on board, and a sermon preached on Sundays, unless bad weather or other extraordinary accidents prevent it.
- Art. III. If any shall be heard to swear, curse or blaspheme the name of God, the Captain is strictly enjoined to punish them for every offence, by causing them to wear a wooden collar or some other shameful badge of distinction, for so long a time as he shall judge proper:—If he be a commissioned officer he shall forfeit one shilling for each offence, and a warrant or inferior officer, six-pence: He who is guilty of drunkenness (if a seaman) shall be put in irons until he is sober, but if an officer, he shall forfeit two days pay.

John Adams wrote both the Article of War and the Rules and Regulations of the Navy.

The Founding Fathers realized that in order to achieve victory over the British the army revolutionary soldiers must not only be strong, but also be God fearing. The way to have God on your side is to obey His commandments and to Worship him.

The Constitution of The United States

The Constitution of The United States has been the supreme law of our nation since the Constitutional Convention in Philadelphia, Pennsylvania adopted it on September 17, 1787. The delegates drafted the document and sent it to Congress for approval. It was then sent to the states to be ratified in the name of "the People." All thirteen states ratified the Constitution by May 29, 1790.

The Constitution provides the framework for the organization of the government. There are three main branches, the Legislative branch, the Executive branch, and the Judicial branch. It carefully outlines the limits of delegated powers that each branch may exercise. It also reserves numerous rights for the individual states, and thus establishes the United States federal system of government.

The Founding Fathers wrote "We the people of the United States" in the preamble to the Constitution, stipulating that the powers to govern belongs to the people who created the government. The preamble established the fact that the federal government has no authority outside of the limited powers given to the three branches.

Much has been said about the Constitution's silence of the subject of God or any Christian reference. The Founders believed that religious matters were best left to the individual citizens. Therefore it is up to each person to teach his children the Gospels. To allow any government to set the agenda for religious instruction, whether it be, local, state, or federal is an infringement on the individual right and responsibility to teach the word of God.

You shall therefore keep His statutes and His commandments which I command you today, that it may go well with you and with your children after you, and that you may prolong your days in the land which the Lord your God is giving you for all time.

–Deuteronomy 4:40 (NKJV)

And Moses called all Israel, and said to them: "Hear O Israel, the statutes and judgments which I speak in your hearing today, that you may learn them and be careful to observe them."

–Deuteronomy 5:1 (NKJV)

The Bill of Rights

During the debates on the adoption of the U. S. Constitution, some of its opponents, including prominent Founding Fathers, were concerned about the failure to protect the basic principles of human liberty. While the Constitution spelled out the government's delegated powers, it did not define the citizen's rights. In their formal ratification of the Constitution, several states either asked for or understood that such amendments would be offered.

The Bill of Rights was introduced by James Madison to the First U.S. Congress in 1791 and came into effect December 15, 1791. In drafting the Bill of Rights, the Framers further defined the role of the federal government by defining certain actions it could not do.

Without the Bill of Rights, basic human rights such as freedom of religion could have potentially been denied or repressed.

The First Amendment states: "Congress shall make no law respecting an establishment of religion, or prohibiting the free exercise thereof...."

The Establishment Clause of the First Amendment prohibits the establishment of a national religion by the Congress, or the preference of one religion over another, non-religion over religion, or religion over non-religion. This is in conjunction with "or prohibiting the free exercise thereof." Clearly this means that the Founding Fathers intended for the government to stay out of religion. The government cannot establishing one, and cannot interfere with the citizens' right to worship as he or she chooses.

After over two hundred years, the United States Supreme Court still frequently hears cases related to the Bill of Rights. In today's courts and culture, interpretation of the First Amendment as an impassable "wall of separation" between church and state. They seek to prohibit religion from entering the halls of government, public schools, and other community areas. Freedom "of religion" lies within the balance. "Freedom *OF* religion" does not mean freedom *FROM* religion.

The government should protect the rights of its citizens to practice their faith in any manner or place they choose. The government cannot prohibit the exercise of religious ceremonies just because it may offend someone. It is our God given right and God given commandment to worship Him when ever we can. The freedom of religion and the exercise thereof is what makes our nation good in the eyes of the Lord.

> *For what great nation is there that has God so near to it, as the Lord our God is to us, for whatever reason we may call upon Him? And what great nation is there that has such statutes and righteous judgments as are in all this law which I set before you this day?*
> **–Deuteronomy 4:7–8 (NKJV)**

> *Therefore if the Son makes you free, you shall be free indeed.*
> **–John 8:36 (NKJV)**

John Jay, our first Chief Justice of the Supreme Court, believed that when we select our national leaders, if we are to preserve our Nation, we must select Christians. He said;

Providence has given to our people the choice of their rulers, and it is the duty, as well as the privilege and interest of our Christian Nation, to select and prefer Christians for their leaders.

Thomas Jefferson wrote in his Bible:

I am a Christian, that is to say a disciple of the doctrines of Jesus. I have little doubt that our whole country will soon be rallied to the unity of our Creator and, I hope, to the pure doctrine of Jesus also.

Now is there any doubt that this great country was founded on Christian principles and Christian ethics?

Freedom Requires Bravery

According to popular legend surrounding the Declaration of Independence, John Hancock signed his name largely and distinctly so King George could read it without his spectacles. While that may not be true, it is true that one of Colonial America's most ardent revolutionaries and rich merchants put his life on the line with his signature. If the revolution was lost or he was caught, he would be hanged by the British.

Certainly, all fifty-six patriots who signed the Declaration of Independence made the same solemn declaration:

> ...with a firm reliance on the protection of Divine Providence, we mutually pledge to each other our lives, our fortunes, and our sacred honor,

John Adams wrote to his wife regarding the meaning of is signature on the document of freedom:

> I am well aware of the toil, and blood, and treasure, that it will cost us to maintain the declaration...I can see that the end is more than worth all the means, and that posterity will triumph in that day's transaction.

A few months before signing the Declaration of Independence, Patrick Henry addressed the Virginia Convention and declared:

> We are not weak if we make a proper use of those means which the God of nature hath placed in our power. Three millions of people, armed in the holy cause of liberty, and in such a country as that which we possess, are invincible by any force which our enemy can send against us. Besides, sir, we shall not fight our battles alone. There is a just God who presides over the destinies of nations, and who will raise up friend to fight our battles for us. The battle, sir, is not to the strong alone; it is to the vigilant, the active and the brave.

> *But if thou shalt indeed obey his voice, and do all that I speak; then I will be an enemy unto thine enemies, and an adversary unto thine adversaries. For mine Angel shall go before thee, and bring thee...."*
> **–Exodus 23:22-23 (KJV)**

United States Capitol Building was used as a church

Many people are surprised to learn that the United States Capitol regularly served as a church building; a practice that began even before Congress officially moved into the building and lasted until well after the Civil War. Below is a brief history of the Capitol's use as a church, and some of the prominent individuals who attended services there.

According to the congressional records for late November of 1800, Congress spent the first few weeks organizing the Capitol rooms, committees, locations, etc. Then, on December 4, 1800, Congress approved the use of the Capitol building as a church building.

The approval of the Capitol for church was given by both the House and the Senate, with House approval being given by Speaker of the House, Theodore Sedgwick, and Senate approval being given by the President of the Senate, Thomas Jefferson. Interestingly, Jefferson's approval came while he was still officially the Vice- President but after he had just been elected president.

Significantly, the Capitol building had been used as a church even for years *before* it was occupied by Congress. The cornerstone for the Capitol had been laid on September 18, 1793; two years later while still under construction, the July 2, 1795, *Federal Orrery* newspaper of Boston reported:

> City of Washington, June 19. It is with much pleasure that we discover the rising consequence of our infant city. Public worship is now regularly administered at the Capitol, every Sunday morning, at 11 o'clock by the Reverend Mr. Ralph.

The reason for the original use of the Capitol as a church might initially be explained by the fact that there were no churches in the city at that time. Even a decade later in 1803, U. S. Senator John Quincy Adams confirmed: "There is no church of any denomination in this city." The absence of churches in Washington eventually changed, however. As one Washington citizen reported: "For several years after the seat of government was fixed at Washington, there were but two small [wooden] churches… Now, in 1837 there are twenty two churches of brick or stone." Yet, even after churches began proliferating across the city, religious services still continued at the Capitol until well after the Civil War and Reconstruction.[13]

It is no exaggeration to say that on Sundays in Washington during the administrations of Thomas Jefferson (1801-1809) and of James Madison (1809–1817) the state became the church. Within a year of his inauguration, Jefferson began attending church services in the House of Representatives. Madison followed Jefferson's example, although unlike Jefferson, who rode on horseback to church in the Capitol, Madison came in a coach. Worship services in the House—a practice that continued until after the Civil War—were acceptable to Jefferson because they were nondiscriminatory and voluntary. Preachers of every Protestant denomination appeared. (Catholic priests began officiating in 1826.) As early as January 1806 a female evangelist, Dorothy Ripley, delivered a camp meeting-style exhortation in the House to Jefferson, Vice President Aaron Burr, and a "crowded audience." Throughout his administration Jefferson permitted church services in executive branch buildings. The Gospel was also preached in the Supreme Court chambers.

Jefferson's actions may seem surprising because his attitude toward the relation between religion and government is usually thought to have been embodied in his recommendation that there exist "a wall of separation between church and state." In that statement, Jefferson was apparently declaring his opposition, as Madison had done in introducing the Bill of Rights, to a "national" religion. In attending church services on public property, Jefferson and Madison were consciously, deliberately, and personally offering symbolic support to religion.[14]

THE FOUNDING FATHERS

George Washington—1st President of the United States (1732–1799)
The American Moses

In 1753, at the age of twenty-one and with no previous military experience, he became a major in the Virginia militia during the French and Indian Wars. Within two years, he was in command of all the Virginia forces. In 1758, he was elected to the Virginia House of Burgesses and left the army in order to serve in the House from 1759–1774.

In 1775, Washington was appointed military advisor for New York and was charged with defending New York from attack by the British. Within weeks, the Second Continental Congress appointed him Commander-in-Chief of the entire military. Washington had not sought the position and he refused payment for it. In 1781, he forced the surrender of Cornwallis at Yorktown and won the war.

In his first general order to his own troops, General Washington said he called on:

Every officer and man...to live, and act, as becomes a Christian Soldier defending the dearest rights and liberties of his country...

In a letter to all state governors in June 1783, he wrote:

I now make it my earnest prayer, that God would have you and the State over which you preside, in his holy protection, that he would incline the hearts of the Citizens to cultivate a spirit of subordination and obedience to Government—to entertain a brotherly affection and love for one another, for their fellow Citizens of the United States at large, and particularly for their Brethren who have served in the Field, and finally, that he would most graciously be pleased to dispose us all, to do Justice, to love Mercy, and to demean ourselves with that Charity, Humility, and Pacific temper of mind which were the Characteristics of the Divine Author of our blessed Religion, and without an humble imitation of whose example in these things, we can never hope to be a Happy Nation.

In 1787, he warned the Constitutional Convention delegates:

If to please the people, we offer what we ourselves disapprove, how can we afterward defend our work? Let us raise a standard to which the wise and the honest can repair; the event is in the Hand of God!

In his famous Inaugural Address to both Houses of Congress, on April 30, 1789, with his hand on a Bible that was opened to Deuteronomy, Chapter 28, he said:

Such being the impressions under which I have, in obedience to the public summons, repaired to the present station, it would be peculiarly improper to omit, in this first official act, my fervent supplications to that Almighty Being who rules over the universe, who presides in the councils of nations and whose providential aides can supply every human defect; that His benediction may consecrate to the liberties and happiness of the people of the United States a government instituted by themselves for these essential purposes; and may enable every instrument employed in its administration to execute with success, the functions allotted to his charge.

In tendering this homage to the Great Author of every public and private good, I assure myself that it expresses your sentiments not less than my own; nor those of my fellow citizens at large, less than either.

No people can be bound to acknowledge and adore the Invisible Hand which conducts the affairs of men more than the people of the United States. Every step by which they have advanced to the character of an independent nation seems to have been distinguished by some token of providential agency.

And in the important revolution just accomplished, in the system of their United government, the tranquil deliberations and voluntary consent of so many distinct communities, from which the event has resulted, can not be compared with the means by which most governments have been established, without some return of pious gratitude, along with an humble anticipation of the future blessings which the past seem to presage...

We ought to be no less persuaded that the propitious smiles of Heaven can never be expected on a nation that disregards the eternal rules of order and right which Heaven itself has ordained; and since the preservation of the sacred fire of liberty and the destiny of the republican model of government are justly considered as deeply, perhaps finally, staked on the experiment.

When he proclaimed a National Day of Thanksgiving, he said:

Whereas it is the duty of all nations to acknowledge the providence of Almighty God, to obey His will, to be grateful for his benefits, and humbly to implore His protection and favor...

Now, therefore, I do recommend and assign Thursday, the twenty-sixth day of November next, to be devoted by the people of these Unites States...that we then may all unite unto him our sincere and humble thanks for His kind care and protection of the people of this country previous to their becoming a nation; for the signal and manifold mercies and the favorable interpositions of His providence in the course and conclusion of the late war; for the great degree of tranquility, union, and plenty which we have since enjoyed; for the peaceable and rational manner in which we have been enabled to establish constitutions of government for our safety and happiness, and particularly the national one now lately instituted; for the civil and religious liberty with which we are blessed...

And also that we may then unite in most humbly offering our prayers and supplications to the great Lord and Ruler of Nations, and beseech Him to pardon our national and other transgressions...to promote the knowledge and practice of the true religion and virtue...

Given under my hand, at the City of New York, the 3rd of October, A.D. 1789.

Beyond his public acclaim, Washington was a man of intense faith. As an elder in his church for almost twenty years, Washington always made God a priority. Many of those around him remarked on the sincerity of the first President's faith in their own journals. Washington was recorded by Henry Cabot Lodge to be a Christian of "simple and childlike faith" with "no doubts or questionings but believing always in an overruling providence and in a merciful God."[15]

The words of his farewell address ring as true today as when he proclaimed, "Reason and experience both forbid us to expect that national morality can exist apart from religious principle."

In 1752, George Washington wrote in his prayer book:

I beseech thee, my sins, remove them from thy presence, as far as the east is from the west, and accept me for the merits of thy Son, Jesus Christ...and as thou wouldst hear me calling upon thee in my prayers, so give me grace to hear thee calling on me in thy Word...Grant that I may hear it with reverence, receive it with meekness, mingle it with faith, and that it may accomplish in me, Gracious God, the good work for which thou has sent it.

Bless, O Lord, all the people of this land, from the highest to the lowest, particularly those whom thou has appointed to rule over us in church and state.

Washington, indisputably a constitutional expert, declared that religion and morality were inseparable from government, and that no patriot, whether politician or clergyman, would attempt to weaken the relationship between government and the influence of religion and morality.[16]

Thomas Jefferson wrote, "…It may truly be said that never did nature and fortune combine more perfectly to make a man great, and to place him in the same constellation with whatever worthies have merited from man an everlasting remembrance."

Just as God had chosen Moses to lead His people out of bondage in Egypt, it could be said that Washington had been chosen to lead the colonists out of bondage from England.

This is why some historians have referred to George Washington as "The American Moses."

Come now therefore, and I will send thee unto Pharaoh, that thou mayest bring forth my people the children of Israel out of Egypt.
–Exodus 3:10 (KJV)

George Washington, in his farewell address as our First President, on September 19, 1796 said:

It is impossible to govern the world without God and the Bible. Of all the dispositions and habits that lead to political prosperity, our religion and morality are the indispensable supporters. Let us with caution indulge the supposition that morality can be maintained without religion. Reason and experience both forbid us to expect that our national morality can prevail in exclusion of religious principle.

Washington was President of the Constitutional Convention of 1787 and served two terms as first President of the United States under the new Constitution. He declined to serve a third term and retired to Mount Vernon in 1797 where he died of pneumonia two years later.

"First in war, first in peace and first in the hearts of his countrymen," said Major General Henry Lee about George Washington, after his death. He was surely that and more. Emerging as the most significant leader in the founding of the United States, he was the essential man, the American Moses, the Father of our Country.[17]

Thomas Jefferson also wrote of Washington: "His integrity was most pure, his justice the most inflexible I have ever known. No motives of friendship or hatred being able to bias his decision. He was indeed, in every sense of the word, a wise, a good, and a great man...[18]

Patrick Henry (1736–1799)

Patrick Henry was one of the most passionate and fiery advocates of the American Revolution and Republicanism. During the Second Virginia Convention's debates on whether to declare independence or negotiate with the British, he rose up on March 23, 1775, and declared, "Should I keep back my opinions at such a time, ... I should consider myself as guilty of treason toward my country, and of an act of disloyalty toward the Majesty of Heaven, which I revere above all earthly kings." Then he called upon his countrymen to trust God and use all the means that He had placed in their power: "Three million of people, armed in the holy cause of liberty, and in such a country as that we possess, are invincible by any force which our enemy can send us. Besides, sirs, we shall not fight our battles alone. There is a just God who presides over the destines of nations, and who will rise up friends to fight our battles for us. The battle, sir, is not to the strong alone; it is to the vigilant, the active and the brave."

Patrick Henry is best know for his quote, "Give me liberty or give me death." Our schools have chosen to eliminate his entire speech from the current textbooks with the exception of his famous line. His 1775 speech reads as follows:

> An appeal to arms and the God of host is all that is left us. But we shall not fight our battle alone. There is a just God that presides over the destinies of nations. The battle is not of the strong alone. Is life so dear or peace so sweet as to be purchased at the price of chains and slavery? Forbid it almighty God. I know not what course others may take, but as for me, give me liberty or give me death.

That was Patrick Henry's speech!

Patrick Henry, a true American Patriot and Revolutionary War leader, who pushed through the "Stamp Act Resolves" in May 1765, the most anti-British political action to that point said:

Whether this will prove a blessing or a curse will depend upon the use our people make of the blessings, which a gracious God hath bestowed on us. If they are wise, they will be great and happy. If they are of a contrary character, they will be miserable.

Righteousness alone can exalt them as a nation. Reader! Whoever thou art, remember this, and in thy sphere practice virtue thyself, and encourage it in others

He further quoted the following passage from the Scripture:

Righteousness exalts a nation, But sin is a reproach to any people
–Proverbs 14:34 (KJV)

Did Patrick Henry believe in God? In 1777 he wrote the following:

It cannot be emphasized too strongly or too often that this great nation was founded not by religionists, but by Christians; not on religion, but on the Gospel of Jesus Christ. For that reason alone, people of other faiths have been afforded freedom of worship here.

Patrick Henry was trying to influence the thinking of an entire population, so why would he continually invoke the name of God, if he weren't addressing religious people?

Patrick Henry believed God had blessed America. He believed we should live righteously. He believed in a gracious God. He warned Americans they would be miserable if they acted contrary to God's word. He believed that Americans must be willing to stand for righteousness at any cost.

John Adams—2nd President of the United States (1735–1826)

John Adams was born in 1735 in the Massachusetts Bay Colony. He was a Harvard-educated lawyer, and a delegate to both the First and Second Continental Congresses. A leader in the independence movement, he served diplomatically in France and Holland during the Revolutionary War. He was instrumental in negotiating the Treaty of Paris, which ended the Revolutionary War.

On April 18, 1775, a British soldier ordered John Adams, John Hancock, and others to "disperse in the name of George the Sovereign King of England. Adams responded to him, *"We recognize no sovereign but God, and no king but Jesus!"*

On March 6, 1789, President Adams called for a national day of fasting and prayer for the country saying:

Call to mind our numerous offenses against the most high God, confess them before Him with the sincerest penitence, implore his pardoning mercy, through the Great Mediator and Redeemer, for our past transgression, and that through the grace of His Holy Spirit, we may be disposed and enabled to yield a more suitable obedience...

In an October 13, 1789 address to the military, that was said by President Adams:

We have no government armed with power capable of contending with human passions unbridled by morality and religion. Avarice, ambition, revenge, or gallantry would break the strongest cords of our Constitution as whale goes through a net. Our Constitution was made only for a moral and religious people. It is wholly inadequate to the government of any other.

In a letter to Thomas Jefferson dated June 28, 1813, Adams said: "The general principles on which the fathers achieved independence were the general principles of Christianity"

John Adams became close friends with Dr. Benjamin Rush, known as the "Father of American Medicine" and signer of the Declaration of Independence. At a point in the Revolutionary War when things weren't going well for the colonists, America was losing more battles than they were winning. With such a bleak prospect of success, Dr. Rush asked John Adams if he thought America could win the war. Adam's answer was clear and unequivocal. He confidently replied: "Yes!—if we fear God and repent our sins."[19]

Only let your conduct be worthy of the gospel of Christ..."..."and not in any way terrified by your adversaries, which is to them a proof of perdition, but to you of salvation.

–Philippians 1:27-28 (NKJV)

Thomas Jefferson—3rd President of the United States (1743–1826)

Thomas Jefferson attended William and Mary College where he studied math, science, literature, philosophy, and law. In April 1767, he was admitted to the Virginia bar. He soon became known as a champion of independence from England. In 1775, he was appointed to the First Continental Congress, and in 1776, the Second Continental Congress which chose him to author the Declaration of Independence. He served in the Virginia House of Delegates, and he was the governor of Virginia during the Revolutionary War.

Raised Episcopalian, Jefferson believed that the New Testament had been polluted by early Christians eager to make Christianity palatable to pagans. He believed that they had mixed the words of Jesus with the teachings of Plato and the philosophy of the ancient Greeks. The authentic words of Jesus were still there, he assured his friend, John Adams. He determined to extract the "authentic" words of Jesus from the rubble, which he believed surrounded His real words.

Jefferson authored a work to bring Christianity to the Indians called "The Life and Morals of Jesus of Nazareth" which set forth the teachings of Jesus from the Gospels. (Today, inappropriately called the "Jefferson Bible")

Jefferson as President of The United States approved several measures appropriating funds to pay for Christian missions to the Indians.

In 1803, at the request of President Thomas Jefferson, the United States Congress allocated federal funds for the salary of a preacher and the construction of his church. That same year, Congress, again at Jefferson's request, ratified a treaty with the Kaskaskia Indians. Congress recognized that most of the members of the tribe had been converted to Christianity, and Congress gave a subsidy of $100.00 a year for seven years for the support of a priest so that he could "instruct as many... children as possible."

Jefferson's treaty with the Kaskaskia Indians provided annual cash support for the Tribe's Roman Catholic priest and church. The treaty stated in part: "And whereas, the greater part of the Tribe have been baptized and received into the Catholic church, to which they are much attached, the United States will give annually for seven years hundred dollars towards the support of a priest of that religion... and...three hundred dollars to assist the said Tribe in the erecting of a church."

Thomas Jefferson also approved federal money for Christian missionary work with the Wyandot tribe in 1807 and the Cherokee Tribe in 1806.

In 1787 an Act of Congress ordained special lands "for the sole use of Christian Indians" and reserved lands for the Moravian Brethren "for civilizing the Indians and promoting Christianity." Congress extended this act three times during Jefferson's presidency, and all three times Jefferson signed the extensions into law.

Written in the front of his personal Bible Jefferson had this statement:

I am a real Christian, that is to say, a disciple of the doctrines of Jesus. I have little doubt that our whole country will soon be rallied to the unity of our creator.

On April 21, 1803, Jefferson wrote this to Dr. Benjamin Rush (also a signer of the Declaration of Independence):

My views...are the result of a life of inquiry and reflection, and very different from the anti-Christian system imputed to me by those who know nothing of my opinions. To the corruptions of Christianity I am, indeed, opposed; but not to the genuine precepts of Jesus himself. I am a Christian in the only sense in which He wished any one to be; sincerely attached to his doctrines in preference to all others.

In that same letter, he wrote:

To the corruptions of Christianity I am, indeed opposed; but not to the genuine precepts of Jesus himself. I am a Christian, in the only sense in which he wished any one to be; sincerely attached to his doctrines, in preference to all others.

March 21, 1804 Sister Marie Therese Farjon of the Ursuline Sisters wrote to Jefferson about their concerns regarding the church property in New Orleans since the United States recently acquired it via the "Louisiana Purchase:"

Please, give us assurance that the spirit of justice which characterizes the United States of America will guarantee that the Sisters would have the continued enjoyment of their present property. And, please, she added, "put [it] officially in writing."

On May 14, 1804, Jefferson responded:

The principles of the constitution and the government of the United States are a sure guarantee [that your property] will be preserved to you sacred and inviolate, and that your institution will be permitted to govern itself according to its own voluntary rules, without interference from the civil authority." He then offered more: "be assured [your religious institution] will meet all the protection which my office can give it.

This remarkable letter, omitted from some of the better known collections of Jefferson's papers, constitutes one of the clearest statements from the founding generation about the freedom of the church. This freedom, often identified as the Doctrine of Church Autonomy and, in earlier times, as the Abstention Doctrine was more fully articulated in the *Watson v. Jones*, 80 U.S. (13 Wall.) 679 (1871) and the over one thousand published precedents relying upon it.[20]

In a letter to William Short on October 31, 1819, he wrote: "But the greatest of all the reformers of the depraved religion of His own country, was Jesus of Nazareth."

But these are written, that ye might believe that Jesus is the Christ, the Son of God; and that believing ye might have life through his name.
–John 20:31 (KJV)

Jefferson also wrote:

He who permits himself to tell a lie once, finds it much easier to do a second and third time, till at length it becomes habitual; he tells lies without attending to it, and truths without the world's believing him. This falsehood of the tongue leads to that of the heart, and in time depraves all its good dispositions.

...and all liars shall have their part in the lake which burns with fire...
–Revelations 21:8 (KJV)

Does all of this sound like the man many current scholars call a "deist" or "atheist" or "an enemy of Christianity"? On the contrary, many of the writings of Thomas Jefferson show without a doubt he was a Christian and was determined to have our country go down the path of Christianity and therefore to salvation.

James Madison (1751–1836)

James Madison, co-author of the "Federalist Papers," was an Episcopalian and trained for the ministry with the Rev. Dr. John Witherspoon. He was a member of the Virginia legislature from 1776-80 and 1784-86, of the Continental Congress in 1780-83, and the Constitutional Convention in 1787. It was in that Convention that he earned the title "Father of the Constitution."

He was a sponsor of the Bill of Rights while a member of the House of Representatives from 1789 to 1797, and authored the Virginia Resolutions of 1798 in opposition to the Alien and Sedition Act. He was Secretary of State from 1801 to 1809, 4th President of the United States from 1809 to 1817, and rector of the University of Virginia for ten years beginning in 1826. He wrote a letter to William Bradford on November 9, 1772:

> A watchful eye must be kept on ourselves lest while we are building ideal monuments of Renown and Bliss here we neglect to have our names enrolled in the Annals of Heaven.

In September of 1773, he wrote in another letter to William Bradford:

> I have sometimes thought there could be no stronger testimony in favor of Religion or against temporal Enjoyments even the most rational and manly than for men who occupy the most honorable and gainful departments and are rising in reputation and wealth, publicly to declare their unsatisfactoriness by becoming fervent Advocates in the cause of Christ, & I wish you may give in your Evidence in this way.

Madison was a member of the committee that authored the 1776 Virginia Bill of Rights and approved of its clause declaring that,

It is the mutual **duty** of all to practice Christian forbearance, love, and charity toward each other (emphasis added)

Madison proposed the wording for the First Amendment that demonstrates that he opposed only the establishment of a federal denomination, not public religious activities. His proposal declared:

The civil rights of none shall be abridged on account of religious belief or worship, nor shall any **_national religion_** be established. (emphasis added)

In 1778, Madison addressed the General Assembly of the State of Virginia:

We have staked the whole future of American civilization, not upon the power of government, far from it. We've staked the future of all our political institutions upon our capacity...to sustain ourselves according to the Ten Commandments of God.

In 1785, in Memorial and Remonstrance Against Religious Assessments, Madison wrote following:

It is the duty of every man to render to the Creator such homage. Before any man can be considered as a member of Civil Society, he must be considered as a subject of the Governor of the Universe.

We have staked the whole future of American civilization, not upon the power of government, far from it. We have staked the future of all our political institutions upon the capacity of mankind for self-government; upon the capacity of each and all of us to govern ourselves, to control ourselves to sustain ourselves according to the Ten Commandments of God.

Although he did speak of a "wall of separation," it is evident that the purpose of said "wall" was to prevent Congress from passing a national law to establish a national religion.

On the basis of the record of these proceedings in the House of Representatives, James Madison was undoubtedly the most important architect among the Members of the House of the Amendments which became the Bill of Rights, but it was James Madison speaking as an advocate of sensible legislative compromise, not as an advocate of incorporating the Virginia Statute of Religious Liberty into the United States Constitution. During the ratification debate in the Virginia Convention, Madison had actually opposed the idea of any Bill of Rights. His sponsorship of the Amendments in the House was obviously not that of a zealous believer in the necessity of the Religion Clauses, but of one who felt it might do some good, could do no harm, and would satisfy those who had ratified the Constitution on the condition that Congress propose a Bill of Rights. His original language "nor shall any national religion be established" obviously does not conform to the "wall of separation" between church and State idea which latter-day commentators have ascribed to him. His explanation on the floor of the meaning of his language—" that Congress should not establish a religion, and enforce the legal observation of it by law"—is of the same ilk. When he replied to Huntington in the debate over the proposal which came from the Select Committee of the House, he urged that the language "no religion shall be established by law" should be amended by inserting the word "national" in front of the word "religion."

It seems indisputable from these glimpses of Madison's thinking, as reflected by actions on the floor of the House in 1789, that he saw the Amendment as designed to prohibit the establishment of a national religion, and perhaps to prevent discrimination among sects. He did not see it as requiring neutrality on the part of government between religion and irreligion.[21]

In 1789, Madison served on the Congressional committee which authorized, approved, and selected paid Congressional chaplains.

In an 1803 letter objecting to the use of government land for churches, he wrote:

The purpose of separation of church and state is to keep forever from these shores the ceaseless strife that has soaked the soil of Europe in blood for centuries.

Madison, in the habit of making notes in his personal Bible, wrote this in Acts, Chapter 19:

Believers who are in a state of grace, have need of the Word of God for their edification and building up therefore implies a possibility of falling. v. 32.

Grace, it is the free gift of God. Luke. 12. 32-v.32.

Giver more blessed than the receiver. v. 35.

To neglect the means for our own preservation is to tempt God: and to trust to them is to neglect Him. v. 3 & Ch. 27. v. 31.

Humility, the better any man is, the lower thoughts he has of himself. v. 19.

Ministers to take heed to themselves & their flock. v. 28.

The Apostles did greater miracles than Christ, in the matter, not manner, of them. v. 11.

At the Constitutional Convention of 1787, James Madison proposed the plan to divide the central government into three branches. He discovered this model of government from the Perfect Governor, as he read *Isaiah 33:22*

For the LORD is our judge, (Judicial)
the LORD is our lawgiver, (Legislative)
the LORD is our king; (Executive)
He will save us.

In 1812, President Madison signed a federal bill that economically aided the Bible Society of Philadelphia in its goal of the mass distribution of the Bible. "An Act for the relief of the Bible Society of Philadelphia" Approved February 2, 1813 by Congress.

On April 20, 1816, Congress also approved financial relief for the Baltimore and Massachusetts Bible Societies for them to continue operating.

Who did President Madison thank and trust during his First Inaugural Address?

...we have all been encouraged to feel in the guardianship and guidance of that Almighty Being whose power regulates the destiny of nations, whose blessings have been so conspicuously dispensed to this rising Republic, and to whom we are bound to address our devout gratitude for the past, as well as our fervent supplications and best hopes for the future.

With regards to the Judiciary department and laws:

As the courts are generally the last in making the decision [on laws], it results to them, by refusing or not refusing to execute a law, to stamp it with its final character. This makes the Judiciary department paramount in fact to the Legislature, *which was never intended, and can never be proper.*

With regards to public officials:

Madison even desired that all public officials would declare openly and publicly their Christian beliefs and testimony.

I have sometimes thought there could not be a stronger testimony in favor of religion or against temporal enjoyments, even the most rational and manly, than for men who occupy the most honorable and gainful departments and [who] are rising in reputation and wealth, publicly to declare their unsatisfactoriness by becoming fervent advocates in the cause of Christ; and I wish you may give in your evidence in this way.

Judges and officers shalt thou make thee in all thy gates, which the LORD thy God giveth thee, throughout thy tribes: and they shall judge the people with just judgment.

–Deuteronomy 16:18 (KJV)

For their rock is not as our Rock, even our enemies themselves being judges.

–Deuteronomy 32:31 (KJV)

Benjamin Franklin (1706–1790)

Benjamin Franklin (1706-90) was a printer, author, inventor, scientist, philanthropist, statesman, diplomat, and public official. He was the first president of the Pennsylvania Society for Promoting the Abolition of Slavery (1774); a member of the Continental Congress (1775-76) where he signed the Declaration of Independence (1776); a negotiator and signer of the final treaty of peace with Great Britain (1783); and a delegate to the Constitutional Convention where he signed the federal Constitution

(1787); Franklin was one of only six men who signed both the Declaration and the Constitution.

Although one of the least religious of our nation's Founding Fathers, Franklin nonetheless understood how crucial moral and biblical virtues would be to the newborn republic. Appealing to the words of Psalm 127:1, Franklin addressed George Washington and counseled his fellow delegates to beseech the aid of Almighty God before they proceeded further:

> I have lived, sir, a long time, and the longer I live, the more convincing proofs I see of the truth, that God governs in the affairs of men. And if a sparrow cannot fall to the ground without His notice, is it probable that an empire can rise without His aid? We have been assured, sir, in the Sacred Writings, that "except the Lord builds the house, they labor in vain that build it." ...I therefore beg leave to move that henceforth prayers imploring the assistance of Heaven, and its blessings on our deliberations, be held in this assembly every morning before we proceed to business, and that one or more of the clergy of this city be requested to officiate in that service.[22]

Unless the Lord builds the house, They labor in vain who built it; Unless the Lord guards the city, The watchman stays awake in vain.

–Psalm 127:1 (KJV)

Franklin was frequently consulted by Thomas Paine (1736–1809) for advice and suggestions regarding his political writings, and Franklin assisted Paine with some of his famous essays. This letter [1] is Franklin's response to a manuscript Paine sent him that advocated against the concept of a providential God.

> ...I have read your manuscript with some attention. By the argument it contains against a particular Providence, though you allow a general Providence, you strike at the foundations of all religion. For without the belief of a Providence, that takes cognizance of guards, and guides, and may favor particular persons, there is no motive to worship a Deity, to fear displeasure, or to pray for his protection...were you to succeed, do you imagine any good would be done by it? You yourself may find it easy to live a virtuous life, without assistance afforded by religion...But think

how great a portion of mankind consists of weak and ignorant men and women, and of inexperienced, inconsiderate youth of both sexes, who have need of the motives of religion to restrain them from vice...which is a great point for its security...If men are so wicked with religion, what would they be if without it? [23]

He wrote his own epitaph:

The body of Benjamin Franklin, printer, like the cover of an old book, its contents torn out, stripped of its lettering, and guilding, lies here, food for worms. But the work shall not be lost; for it will, as he believed, appear once more in a new and more elegant edition, revised and corrected by the Author.

Samuel Adams (1722–1803)

Samuel Adams was born in Boston, Massachusetts on September 27, 1722... He was a leader of the fight against British Colonial rule, and a signer of the Declaration of Independence. Adams was a cousin of John Adams who became the second President of the United States.

Adams' father, a deacon of a church and successful brewer, played a prominent role in Boston politics. When Samuel was a young man, the royal government ruled the senior Adams' investments illegal, ruining him financially. This may have been the cause of Samuel's animosity toward, and opposition to, Colonial authority.

Samuel Adams graduated in 1743 from Harvard College with a Master of Arts degree. After college he entered private business, and throughout this period was an outspoken participant in Boston town meetings. When his business failed in 1764, Adams entered politics full-time and was elected to the Massachusetts legislature. He led the effort to establish a committee of correspondence that published a Declaration of Colonial Rights he had written.

Adams was a vocal opponent of several laws passed by the British Parliament to raise revenue in the American Colonies. By 1773, Adams and his Boston associates had pressured England to rescind all these measures but one, the Tea Act. The Tea Act granted the British East India company a monopoly on the sale of tea to the colonies and included a tax paid to the British crown. Opposition reached its peak on December 16, 1773, when a group of Bostonians dumped a British cargo of tea into Boston Harbor. This act of resistance is referred to as the Boston Tea Party.

In 1774, the Massachusetts legislature sent Adams and four others as its representatives to the First Continental Congress. Adams served Massachusetts again at the Second Continental Congress where he was an advocate for independence and confederation for the American Colonies.

Adams served Continental Congress until his return to Boston in 1781. He initially opposed the new Constitution of the United States but finally supported its ratification in Massachusetts. Adams served as Governor of Massachusetts from 1793 to 1797.[24]

Known as the "Father of the American Revolution" and the "Firebrand of the Revolution," Samuel Adams was arguably the most effective verbal rabble-rouser in American history. He was a leader in the events leading up to the American Revolution, helped to found the Sons of Liberty, formed Boston's Committee of Correspondence, was a member of the first Continental Congress, and signed the Declaration of Independence. He helped to draft the Articles of Confederation and served as president in the Massachusetts Senate before becoming the Lieutenant Governor and subsequently the Governor of Massachusetts.

Samuel Adams was also a steadfast Christian. In "The Rights of the Colonists," which he wrote in 1772, he said following:

> The right to freedom being the gift of the Almighty...The rights of the colonists as Christians...may be best understood by reading and carefully studying the institutions of The Great Law Giver and Head of the Christian Church, which are to be found clearly written and promulgated in the New Testament.

After signing the Declaration of Independence, he proclaimed:

> We have this day restored the Sovereign to whom all men ought to be obedient. He reigns in heaven and from the rising to the setting of the sun, let His kingdom come.

In his February 1795 Proclamation for a Day of Public Fasting, Humiliation and Prayer, then Governor Adams included the following:

That with true repentance and contrition of Heart, we may unitedly implore the forgiveness of our Sins, through the merits of Jesus Christ, and humbly supplicate our Heavenly Father, to grant us the aids of his Grace, for the amendment of our Hearts and Lives, and vouchsafe his smiles upon our temporal concerns.

And finally, these are the words in his Last Will and Testament:

Principally, and first of all, I resign my soul to the Almighty Being who gave it, and my body I commit to the dust, relying on the merits of Jesus Christ for the pardon of my sins.

Alexander Hamilton (1755 – 1804)

Alexander Hamilton was secretary and aide-de-camp to George Washington from 1777 to 1781. He was a member of the Continental Congress from 1782-83 and from 1787-88. In 1787, he was a representative to the Constitutional Convention. He was the first United States Secretary of the Treasury, and ran for the presidency against Aaron Burr in 1800 and then for Governor of New York in 1804.

Hamilton, who regularly led his household in prayer, also wrote about the connection between Christianity and political freedom. He helped to form an organization that would support Christianity and the United States Constitution, named the Christian Constitutional Society. In an 1802 letter to co-founder James Bayard, he said:

I now offer you the outline of the plan they have suggested. Let an association be formed to be denominated 'The Christian Constitutional Society,' its object to be first: The support of the Christian religion. Second: The support of the United States Constitution.

I have carefully examined the evidences of the Christian religion, and if I was sitting as a juror upon its authenticity I would unhesitatingly give my verdict in its favor. I can prove its truth as clearly as any proposition ever submitted to the mind of man.

After the Constitutional Convention of 1787, Hamilton stated:

> For my own part, I sincerely esteem it a system which without the finger of God, never could have been suggested and agreed upon by such a diversity of interests.

Because of a political rivalry, Alexander Hamilton died in a dual with Aaron Burr in July 1804. His last words were:

> I have a tender reliance on the mercy of the Almighty, through the merits of the Lord Jesus Christ. I am a sinner. I look to Him for mercy; pray for me.

Alexander Hamilton, being a devout Christian, truly believed the founding of America, the writing of the Declaration of Independence, and the Constitution of the United States were the result of divine intervention.

...written with the finger of God...

–Deuteronomy 9:10 (KJV)

John Hancock (1737–1793)

Once the wealthiest merchant in Boston, John Hancock was groomed by Sam Adams and became one of the leading players in the Revolution. He presided over the Second Continental Congress. He was the first elected governor of Massachusetts and was reelected eight times. He was reelected President of the Second Continental Congress after the ratification of the Articles of Confederation and presided over the Massachusetts convention which ratified the Constitution of the United States. John Hancock's signature is the largest on the Declaration of Independence.

On April 15, 1775, four days before the "Shot Heard 'Round the World," he wrote:

> In circumstances dark as these, it becomes us, as Men and Christians, to reflect that, whilst every prudent Measure should be taken to ward off the impending Judgments...

All confidence must be withheld from the Means we use; and reposed only on that GOD who rules in the Armies of Heaven, and without whose Blessing the best human Counsels are but Foolishness—and all created Power Vanity.

It is the Happiness of his Church that, when the Powers of Earth and Hell combine against it...that the Throne of Grace is of the easiest access—and its Appeal thither is graciously invited by the Father of Mercies, who has assured it, that when his Children ask Bread he will not give them a Stone...

RESOLVED, That it be, and hereby is recommended to the good People of this Colony of all Denominations, that THURSDAY the Eleventh Day of May next be set apart as a Day of Public Humiliation, Fasting and Prayer...to confess the sins...to implore the Forgiveness of all our Transgression...and a blessing on the Husbandry, Manufactures, and other lawful Employments of this People; and especially that the union of the American Colonies in Defense of their Rights (for hitherto we desire to thank Almighty GOD) may be preserved and confirmed...And that AMERICA may soon behold a gracious Interposition of Heaven. By Order of the [Massachusetts] Provincial Congress, John Hancock, President.

With the war underway, Hancock made his way to the Continental Congress in Philadelphia with the other Massachusetts delegates. On May 24, 1775, he was unanimously elected President of the Continental Congress. Hancock was a good choice for president for several reasons. He was experienced, having often presided over legislative bodies and town meetings in Massachusetts. His wealth and social standing inspired the confidence of moderate delegates, while his association with Boston radicals made him acceptable to other radicals. His position was somewhat ambiguous, because the role of the president was not fully defined. Like other presidents of Congress, Hancock's authority was limited to that of a presiding officer. Because he had to handle a great deal of official correspondence, he found it necessary to hire clerks at his own expense to help with the paperwork.

Hancock served in Congress through some of the darkest days of the Revolutionary War. The British drove Washington from New York and New Jersey in 1776, which prompted Congress to flee to Baltimore, Maryland. Hancock and Congress returned to Philadelphia in March 1777, but were compelled to flee six months later when the British occupied Philadelphia. Hancock wrote innumerable letters to Colonial officials, raising money, supplies, and troops for Washington's army. He chaired the Marine Committee and took pride in helping to create a small fleet of American frigates, including the USS *Hancock*, which was named in his honor.

In his last will and testament, John Hancock stated the following:

> I John Hancock, ... being advanced in years and being of perfect mind and memory-thanks be given to God-therefore calling to mind the mortality of my body and knowing it is appointed for all men once to die [Hebrews 9:27], do make and ordain this my last will and testament... Principally and first of all, I give and recommend my soul into the hands of God that gave it: and my body I recommend to the earth ...nothing doubting but at the general resurrection I shall receive the same again by the mercy and power of God...

And as it is appointed unto men once to die, but after this the judgment.
–Hebrews 9:27 (KJV)

Charles Carroll (1737–1832)

Charles Carroll was a leader of the American Revolution and the only Roman Catholic signer of the Declaration of Independence. He helped to draft the Maryland Constitution, was a member of the Committee of Correspondence, the State Council of Safety, and eventually became a United States Senator, where he helped to establish the Bill of Rights.

As a Catholic, he was opposed to support of the Anglican Church and wrote his views in a series of articles in the Maryland Gazette. Carroll also served in the Continental Congress (1776–1778), the Maryland state senate (1777–1800), and the United States senate (1789–1792).

Carroll wrote a letter to John McHenry on November 4, 1800:

> Without morals a republic cannot subsist any length of time; they therefore who are decrying the Christian religion, whose morality

is so sublime & pure, [and] which denounces against the wicked eternal misery, and [which] insured to the good eternal happiness, are undermining the solid foundation of morals, the best security for the duration of free governments.

When the signatories of the Declaration of Independence pledged their "lives, fortunes, and sacred honor," few men had more to lose than Charles Carroll. A wealthy landowner, businessman, and member of a prominent Maryland family, Carroll risked the confiscation of his estate and the loss of his life if the British had prevailed. Yet when asked if he would sign or not, he replied, "Most willingly, and ratified what he called" this record of glory. Reflecting on that act fifty years later, Carroll—by then the last surviving signer—concluded that the civil and religious liberties secured by the Declaration and enjoyed by that present generation were "the best earthly inheritance their ancestors could bequeath to them."

As a Roman Catholic, Carroll also had much to gain. Though many American colonists harbored intense suspicion toward Catholics (it was widely believed that Catholic doctrine was incompatible with republicanism), Carroll and his contemporary co-religionists presciently perceived that the American understanding of liberty entailed not only political and economic freedom but religious freedom as well. Carroll himself held the hope that among sects in the new regime, "no one would be so predominant as to become the religion of the State." He continued, "that hope was thus early entertained because all of them joined in the same cause with few exceptions of individuals." Father John Carroll, Charles's cousin and the first bishop of the United States, agreed: "In 1776, American Independence was declared and a revolution effected, not only in political affairs but also in those relating to Religion. For while the thirteen provinces of North America rejected the yoke of England, they proclaimed, at the same time, freedom of conscience and the right of worshipping the Almighty according to the spirit of the religion to which each one should belong."

In such a context of freedom, Charles Carroll become one of the early Republic's most prominent and respected statesmen. Early in 1776, he joined Samuel Chase, Benjamin Franklin, and Father John Carroll on a diplomatic mission to Catholic Quebec to ask for its aid in the Revolution.[25]

On his 89th birthday, he wrote:

On the mercy of my Redeemer I rely for salvation and on His merits; not on the works I have done in obedience to His precepts.

To obtain religious as well as civil liberty, I entered zealously into the Revolution… God grant that this religious liberty may be preserved in these States, to the end of time, and that all who believe in the religion of Christ may practice the leading principle of charity, the basis of every virtue.

Carroll also wrote:

Without morals a republic cannot subsist any length of time; they therefore who are decrying the Christian religion, whose morality is so sublime and pure…are undermining the solid foundation of morals, the best security for the duration of free governments."

When the righteous are in authority, the people rejoice: but when the wicked beareth rule, the people mourn.

–Proverbs 29:2 (KJV)

Gouverneur Morris (1725–1816)

Of French and English descent, Morris was born at Morrisania estate, in Westchester (present Bronx) County, NY, in 1752. His family was wealthy and enjoyed a long record of public service. His elder half-brother, Lewis, signed the Declaration of Independence.

Gouverneur was educated by private tutors and at a Huguenot school in New Rochelle. In early life, he lost a leg in a carriage accident. He attended King's College (later Columbia College and University) in New York City, graduating in 1768 at the age of 16. Three years later, after reading law in the city, he gained admission to the bar.

When the Revolution loomed on the horizon, Morris became interested in political affairs. Because of his conservatism however, he at first feared the movement, which he believed would bring mob rule. Furthermore, some of his family and many of his friends were Loyalists. But, beginning in 1775, for some reason he sided with the Whigs. That same year, representing Westchester County, he took a seat in New York's Revolutionary provincial congress (1775 to 1777). In 1776, when he also served in the militia, along with John Jay and Robert R. Livingston he drafted the first constitution of the state. Subsequently he joined its council of safety (1777).

From 1777 to 1778 Morris sat in the legislature and from 1778 to 1779 in the Continental Congress, where he numbered among the youngest and most brilliant members. During this period, he signed the Articles of Confederation and drafted instructions for Benjamin Franklin, in Paris, as well as those that provided a partial basis for the treaty ending the War for Independence. Morris was also a close friend of Washington and one of his strongest congressional supporters.

Because of the opposition of Gov. George Clinton's faction, Morris was defeated in his bid for reelection to Congress in 1779. Morris then relocated to Philadelphia and resumed the practice of law. This temporarily removed him from the political scene, but in 1781 he resumed his public career when he became the principal assistant to Robert Morris, Superintendent of Finance for the United States, to whom he was unrelated. Gouverneur held this position for 4 years.

Morris emerged as one of the leading figures at the Constitutional Convention. His speeches, more frequent than those by anyone else, numbered 173. Although sometimes presented in a light vein, they were usually substantive. A strong advocate of nationalism and aristocratic rule, he served on many committees, including those on postponed matters and style, and stood in the thick of the decision making process. Above all, it was apparently he who actually made the original draft of the Constitution.

Gouverneur Morris stated:

Religion is the solid basis of good morals; therefore education should teach the precepts of religion, and the duties of man toward God.

And thou shalt teach them diligently...
–Deuteronomy 6:7 (KJV)

Francis Hopkinson (1737–1791)

Born September 21, 1737 in Philadelphia, Pennsylvania Francis Hopkinson was a graduate of College of Philadelphia. He was a Lawyer, Judge and Author.

Thomas Hopkinson was an intimate friend of Benjamin Franklin and was instrumental in Mr. Franklin's discoveries regarding electricity. Thomas would help to establish the Philadelphia Library, and would be a trustee of the newest college in that city.

In November of 1763, the Surveyor General appointed Francis to be the Collector of the King's Customs at the Port of Salem, in New Jersey. Mr. Hopkinson was ever busy, when not working he spent much of his spare time in service to the Philadelphia Library as secretary from 1759 through 1766 and as Librarian for just a littler more than a year from 1764 to 1765. In his service to God, he taught the children music and Psalms and was appointed church-secretary at Christ Church in 1763. In 1766 Mr. Hopkinson continuing his good work at Christ Church in Philadelphia, along with Edward Duffield took over the responsibilities of overseeing and testing the education of black students both free and slaved; the boys were taught the catechism and to read while the girls were instructed in the catechism, reading, sewing, knitting and marking.

Though Francis was now a successful businessman, a husband, and a new father, he still had the yearning for public service. During the next three and a half years he did not give up his pursuit of a government appointment. Finally, on May 1, 1772, Hopkinson was given the position of Collector of his Majesty's Customs for the Port of New Castle upon Delaware. This added to his already growing wealth, to the extent that he could purchase one thousand and sixty acres of land known as Putney Common, from John Penn, in October of 1772.

Clearly, his musical acumen enraptured many hearts and minds, and his writing accomplishing the same. Mr. Hopkinson's first pamphlet of any renown was "A Pretty Story" which was a political allegory. In September, 1774, which was about the same time the First Continental Congress convened, he published his pamphlet with the full title of: A PRETTY STORY, written in the YEAR OF OUR LORD 1774. By PETER GRIEVOUS, Esq., A.B.C.D.E. The tale was a history of the events that provoked that important Congressional assembly. The story's Preface is so cheerful and charming in tone that the reader would never suspect the solemn purpose of the author.

In his work "On Mottos" Hopkinson revealed himself a man well studied in the Bible; having a clear vision of Scriptural authority, and seeing the human interference and misinterpretation of the Bible. He further demonstrated his knowledge of God's Word in his piece entitled, "On Adversity", by writing,

> When we find that the pleasures of the world cannot give solid, permanent satisfaction-cannot gratify all our desires, we are induced to turn to that only Being who is the source of true felicity, and in whom alone there is fullness of joy. In the time of distress, we feel and know what we only had, perhaps, a transient idea of before, that the Christian graces and virtues are the only true sources of happiness.

Hopkinson further wrote in "On Adversity" that,

> Thus it is that the calamities of life may become real blessings, if a right use be made of them. If the smiles of prosperity do not fill the soul with gratitude, love and religious joy; they will produce arrogance, self-sufficiency and pride: if pain, distress, and disappointment, the loss of those we love, and injuries from those who love not us, no not wean the hear from too strong an attachment to the transitory pleasures of life, and direct our views to better hopes; they will either plunge us in the giddy eddies of vicious enjoyments, to drown every painful sensibility, or will throw the mind into a wicked despondency, and occasion profane murmurings against the Author of our existence, or fix us in a gross and sinful infidelity.

On June 21, 1776, Francis Hopkinson was chosen as one of the delegates to Congress. He signed the Declaration of Independence, and soon after was appointed Judge of Admiralty, for Pennsylvania. When the Constitution was put before the people, Francis gave his full support, with both his voice and his pen.

In 1790 President George Washington appointed Mr. Hopkinson judge of the United States court, for the district of Pennsylvania.

Upon his passing, his mother Mary Hopkinson wrote: "My Dear Son Francis Hopkinson departed this life May the 9th 1791. O my God, grant that he and all that I have lost may be happy in the arms of thy Redeeming Love."

Francis Hopkinson was never known to use a profane word; such was his Christianity and refinement that it was never recounted that he said anything that would have caused a lady to blush. He was quite versatile in his talents, being proficient in mechanics, chemistry, mathematics, music and writing. Beloved son, adoring husband, loving father, a flawed but dependable and service minded Christian, patriot to a young nation; truly, a Founding Father of this country was Francis Hopkinson.[26]

But refuse profane and old wives' fables, and exercise thyself rather unto godliness.

–1Timothy 4:7 (KJV)

John Jay (1745–1829)

John Jay was a member of the Continental Congress from 1774 through 1779, serving as its president in 1778-79. He drafted New York's first constitution in 1777, was the chief justice of the New York supreme court in 1777 and 1778. He became the United States minister to Spain in 1779, and signed the final peace treaty with England. He was the US secretary of foreign affairs 1784 to 1789. He was one of the Constitution's most outspoken proponent, and in 1789, he became the first Chief Justice of the United States Supreme Court and finally, the governor of New York from 1795 until 1801.

The co-author of the Federalist Papers was elected president of the Westchester Bible Society in 1818, and in 1821, John Jay became the president of the American Bible Society.

In December 1776, Jay addressed New York's constitutional convention immediately following the American defeat at Long Island, Manhattan, and White Plains. He told the audience of Americans disillusioned by their losses and questioning the moral righteousness of their cause,

The Gospel is yet to be preached to those western Regions, & we have the highest Reason to believe that the Almighty will not suffer Slavery & the Gospel to go Hand in Hand. It cannot, it will not be.

In April 1794, in a letter to his wife, Sally, John Jay wrote: "God's will be done; to him I resign—in him I confide. Do the like. Any other philosophy applicable to this occasion is delusive. Away with it."

In a letter to Jedidiah Morse, in 1797, he wrote:

It is to be regretted, but so I believe the fact to be, that except the Bible there is not a true history in the world. Whatever may be the virtue, discernment, and industry of the writers, I am persuaded that truth and error (though in different degrees) will imperceptibly become and remain mixed and blended until they shall be separated forever by the great and last refining fire.

Now, one could argue that the first Chief Justice of the United States of America is likely to have had a better idea than any of our current Justices as to the intent of the Founding Fathers, since he was one and knew most of them.

In 1811, in a letter to John Bristed, he wrote:

I do not recollect to have had more than two conversations with atheists about their tenents. The first was this: I was at a large party, of which were several of that description. They spoke freely and contemptuously of religion. I took no part in the conversation. In the course of it, one of them asked me if I believed in Christ. I answered that I did, and that I thanked God that I did.

On October 12, 1816, John Jay said:

Providence has given to our people the choice of their rulers, and it is the duty, as well as the privilege and interest of our Christian nation to select and prefer Christians for their rulers. National prosperity can neither be obtained nor preserved without the favor of Providence.

By me princes rule, and nobles, even all the judges of the earth.
–Proverbs 8:16 (KJV)

John Marshall (1755–1835)

John Marshall served as an officer in the Continental Army from 1775 until 1779, where he became a devoted fan of General George Washington. His admiration prompted him to write a biography of Washington. He became a lawyer in 1780 and was elected to the Virginia House of Delegates in 1782, 1787, and 1795. He was a champion of the Constitution at the Virginia ratifying convention in 1788, earning the gratitude of his hero, Washington.

He was appointed one of three envoys sent on a diplomatic mission to France in 1797. Although offered appointment to the United States Supreme Court in 1798, Marshall preferred to remain in private practice.

John Marshall was elected to the United States House of Representatives in 1799, and in 1800 President John Adams appointed him Secretary of State. The next year, President Adams nominated him Chief Justice of the United States Supreme Court, and the Senate confirmed the appointment on January 27, 1801. He continued to serve as Secretary of State throughout President Adams's term and continued in both positions for a brief time following President Thomas Jefferson's inauguration.

In a letter to Jasper Adams on May 9, 1833, Chief Justice Marshall wrote:

The American population is entirely Christian, and with us Christianity and Religion are identified. It would be strange indeed, if with such a people, our institutions did not presuppose Christianity, and did not often refer to it, and exhibit relations with it.

Open thy mouth, judge righteously, and plead the cause of the poor and needy.
–Proverbs 31:9 (KJV)

Marshall served as Chief Justice for 34 years, the longest tenure of any Chief Justice. With the Marbury v. Madison case, he helped establish the Supreme Court as the final authority on the meaning of the Constitution. Marshall died on July 6, 1835, at the age of 79.

George Mason (1725–1835)

George Mason, the principal author of the Bill of Rights, was a well-to-do Virginia farmer, lawyer, judge, and politician. In 1749 he served as a justice of the Fairfax County Court, and in 1775-76 was a representative to the temporary government of the state of Virginia, the Virginia Convention. He is best known as the author of the Virginia Declaration of Rights, which spelled out the concept that men are, by nature, free and that they have inherent rights.

Mason was a delegate to the Constitutional Convention in Philadelphia, although he was adamantly opposed to the final version of the Constitution which was approved by the other delegates, believing that the Convention was giving Congress too much power over the states. He believed that the President and Senate together would form a pseudo-monarchy. "The executive and legislative powers," he said, "thus connected, will destroy all balances."

The Constitution, Mason believed, provided no security against the powers of government being appropriated by a single faction. He became a major anti-federalist and argued against ratification of the Constitution.

In his will, George Mason wrote:

> My soul I resign into the hands of my Almighty Creator, whose tender mercies are all over His works, who hateth nothing that He hath made, and to the justice and wisdom of whose dispensations I willingly and cheerfully submit, humbly hoping from His unbounded mercy and benevolence, through the merits of my blessed Savior, a remission of my sins.

Thomas McKean (1734–1817)

Thomas McKean, signer of the Declaration of Independence, studied for seven years at Reverend Francis Alison's academy and was admitted to the Delaware bar in 1754, at the age of 20. He soon went into business for himself and opened branches in Delaware, Pennsylvania, and New Jersey. He later became a deputy attorney general of Sussex County and a member of the legislature.

He became involved in the Revolution in 1765 when he became a delegate to the Stamp Act Congress. Because he was absent when the Declaration of Independence was signed, he affixed his signature later.

Thomas McKean was a member of the Continental Congress 1774-76 and 1778-83, serving as president thereof in 1781; was simultaneously president (as the governor was then known) of Delaware in 1777 as well as chief justice of Pennsylvania from that year until 1799; and served three consecutive terms as governor of Pennsylvania 1799 to 1808. He helped to frame the Delaware constitution, supported and signed the Articles of Confederation, and was a member of Pennsylvania's state constitutional convention

On July 10, 1791, Thomas McKean was elected as the second President of the United States in Congress Assembled, and in 1792, along with James Wilson, he wrote "Commentaries on the Constitution" of the United States.

As Chief Justice, McKean heard the case Respublica vs. John Roberts. Roberts was found guilty of treason and was condemned to death. When he had only a few days before his execution, McKean called the condemned man back to the bench and said this to him:

You will probably have but a short time to live. Before you launch into eternity, it behooves you to improve the time that may be allowed you in this world. It behooves you most seriously to reflect upon your conduct, to repent of your evil deeds, to be incessant in prayers to the great and merciful God to forgive your manifold transgressions and sins, to teach you to rely upon the merit and passion of a dear Redeemer and thereby to avoid those regions of sorrow, those doleful shades where peace and rest can never dwell, where even hope cannot enter. It behooves you to seek the fellowship, advice and prayers of pious and good men, to be persistent at the throne of grace and to learn the way that leadeth to happiness. May you reflecting upon these things and pursuing the will of the great Father of Light and Life, be received into the company and society of angels and archangels and the spirits of just men made perfect and may you be qualified to enter into the joys of heaven, joys unspeakable and full of glory.

Imagine today having a judge tell a condemned man to repent so he may have everlasting life with Jesus Christ in heaven. This was when all of our leaders and judges prayed for guidance and wisdom from our Lord. This was a time when America was a "Christian Nation!"

Dr. Benjamin Rush (1746–1813)

Dr. Benjamin Rush, though not one of the more famous of the Founding Fathers was, along with George Washington and Benjamin Franklin, arguably one of America's three most noteworthy men of the new nation. He was a signer of the Declaration of Independence, helped found five colleges, served under three presidents, and personally trained more than 3,000 medical students. He is also the founder of the Sunday School movement in America as well as the first Bible society in America. He published the first American textbook on chemistry. He was active in the Sons of Liberty in Philadelphia.

In June 1776, he was elected to attend the provincial conference to send delegates to the Continental Congress and was appointed to represent Philadelphia. In 1777, he became surgeon-general in the Continental Army but became critical of the administration of the army medical service and Dr. William Shippen, who was in charge of it. He complained directly to General George Washington who deferred to Congress. Congress supported Dr. Shippen, and Dr. Rush resigned in disgust.

As the war continued and Army forces under General Washington suffered a series of defeats, Rush secretly campaigned for removal of Washington as commander in chief, and went so far as to write an anonymous letter to then Governor Patrick Henry of Virginia. He was caught in the act and confronted by Washington, at which point he bowed out of any activities related to the war. He later regretted his criticism of Washington and realized what a great leader he was. In 1789, he wrote in newspapers of Philadelphia advocating the adoption of the federal Constitution. He was elected to the Pennsylvania convention and had a hand in adopting it. From 1797 to 1813, he was treasurer of the US Mint.

Because of his Christian beliefs, Benjamin Rush was concerned about the possible corruption of elected officials of the new government that he wrote a letter to Thomas Jefferson that stated:

> I have always considered Christianity as the strong ground of republicanism. The spirit is opposed, not only to splendor, but even to the very forms of monarchy, and many of its precepts have for their

objects republican liberty and equality as well as simplicity, integrity, and economy in government. It is only necessary for republicanism to ally itself to the Christian religion to overturn all the corrupted political and religious institutions in the world.

While they promise them liberty, they themselves are the servants of corruption: for of whom a man is overcome, of the same is he brought in bondage.

–2 Peter 2:19 (KJV)

On March 28, 1787, he wrote an open letter "To the citizens of Philadelphia: A Plan for Free Schools".

Let the children...be carefully instructed in the principles and obligations of the Christian religion. This is the most essential part of education. The great enemy of the salvation of man, in my opinion, never invented a more effectual means of extirpating Christianity from the world than by persuading mankind that it was improper to read the Bible at schools.

He continued in the same letter:

The only foundation for a useful education in a republic is to be laid in religion. Without this there can be no virtue, and without virtue there can be no liberty.

"Come, ye children, hearken unto me: I will teach you the fear of the LORD.

–Psalm 34:11 (KJV)

Roger Sherman (1721–1793)

Roger Sherman rose from justice of the peace and county judge to an associate judge of the Connecticut Superior Court and to representative in both houses of the Colonial assembly. Although opposed to extremism, he promptly joined the fight against Britain. He supported non-importation measures and headed the New Haven committee of correspondence.

Sherman was a longtime and influential member of the Continental Congress (1774 to 1781 and 1783 to 1784). He won membership on the committees that drafted the Declaration of Independence and the Articles of Confederation, as well as those concerned with Indian affairs, national finances, and military matters. To solve economic problems, at both national and state levels, he advocated high taxes rather than excessive borrowing or the issuance of paper currency.

Roger Sherman is the only of the Founding Fathers who signed all four of America's founding documents: Articles of Association (1774), Declaration of Independence (1776), Articles of Confederation (1778), and the United States Constitution (1787).

It is because of Sherman that we have two legislative bodies; it was his idea to create both the House and the Senate in order to resolve conflict between the big and small states.

In a letter to Samuel Hopkins, June 28, 1790, he said:

I admit that it is the duty of all to acknowledge that the divine law which requires us to love God with all our heart and our neighbor as ourselves, on pain of eternal damnation is holy, just and good; and I suppose that the conscience of every sinner who shall be finally condemned by the law, will witness to the justice of the sentence...

Sherman also wrote:

Let us live no more to ourselves, but to Him who loved us, and gave Himself to die for us.

All civil rights and the right to hold office were to be extended to persons of any Christian denomination.

Also a theologian, he wrote a personal creed which was adopted by his church:

I believe that there is one only living and true God, existing in three persons, the Father, the Son, and the Holy Ghost, the same in substance, equal in power and glory. That the Scriptures of the Old and New Testaments are a revelation from God, and a complete rule to direct us how we may glorify and enjoy Him.

Roger Sherman was a Bible believing Christian and as such he made every effort to insure Christian values were part of the founding of this nation, to be an example to the rest of the world.

> *Go ye therefore, and teach all nations, baptizing them in the name of the Father, and of the Son, and of the Holy Ghost.*
> —**Matthew 28:19 (KJV)**

Noah Webster (1758–1843)

Noah Webster, the Father of American Education, was a revolutionary soldier, judge, legislator, American Founder, and the creator of Webster's Dictionary. He served nine terms in the Connecticut General Assembly, three terms in the Massachusetts Legislature, and four years as a judge. One of the first Founding Fathers to call for a Constitutional Convention, he was also one of the most active in the ratification of the Constitution.

He strongly believed that all Americans should speak the same language, and he was quite concerned about spelling and pronunciation. Hence, he compiled the first American dictionary. His first edition was published in 1806 with thirty seven thousand words. He published two more the following year. He spent the rest of his life cataloguing words. In 1828, he completed his final dictionary, one with seventy thousand words. He used words like "color" instead of "colour," and "magic" instead of "magick" and added uniquely American words such as "skunk," "hickory," and "chowder."

On December 20, 1808, he wrote in a letter to Thomas Dawes:

> About a year ago, an unusual revival of religion took place in New Haven... and I was lead by a spontaneous impulse of repentance, prayer, and entire submission of myself to my Maker and Redeemer. In the month of April last, I made a profession of faith." This unusual revival was a part of the Great Awakening that shook America in the early 19th Century.

As evidenced in his textbook, "History of the United States, published in 1832, he believed that Christianity and government could not and should not be separated:

The religion which has introduced civil liberty is the religion of Christ and His apostles, which enjoins humility, piety, and benevolence; which acknowledges in every person, a brother or a sister, and a citizen with equal rights. This is genuine Christianity, and to this we owe our free constitutions of government.

Almost all the civil liberty now enjoyed in the world owes its origin to the principles of the Christian religion.

It is the sincere desire of the writer that our citizens should early understand that the genuine source of correct republican principles is the Bible...

The moral principles and precepts contained in the Scriptures ought to form the basis of all of our civil constitutions and laws...All the miseries and evils which men suffer from vice, crime, ambition, injustice, oppression, slavery, and war, proceed from their despising or neglecting the precepts contained in the Bible.

Noah Webster is also quoted as saying:

Every civil government is based upon some religion or philosophy of life. Education in a nation will propagate the religion of that nation. In America, the foundational religion was Christianity. And it was sown in the hearts of Americans through the home and private and public schools for centuries. Our liberty, growth, and prosperity was the result of a Biblical philosophy of life. Our continued freedom and success is dependent on our educating the youth of America in the principles of Christianity.

And ye shall teach them your children, speaking of them when thou sittest in thine house, and when thou walkest by the way, when thou liest down, and when thou risest up."
—Deuteronomy 11:19 (KJV)

If thy children will keep my covenant and my testimony that I shall teach them, their children shall also sit upon thy throne for evermore.
—Psalms 132:12 (KJV)

The founding of our country was in no doubt the work of almighty God. All you have to do is read the writings or our Founding Fathers. They had established a bond with God to create a sanctuary for the Godly against the pressures of the ungodly. This shows how the founding of our nation was approved and ordained by God. Our leaders were for the most part very devout Christians. Modern history has tried to distort the truth by ignoring the writings of people like Thomas Jefferson who wrote in his own personal Bible *"I am a real Christian…"*. These "new historians" define Jefferson a "deist" or "anti-Christian". Well who do you believe, people who are trying to re-write history or Thomas Jefferson in his own words? (emphasis added)

These same "historians" claim Benjamin Franklin was anti-Christian and had no use for the Bible or prayer. Just look at Mr. Franklin's own words:

I have lived, sir, a long time, and the longer I live, the more convincing proofs I see of the truth, that God governs in the affairs of men…I therefore beg leave to move that henceforth prayers imploring the assistance of Heaven, and its blessings on our deliberations, be held in this assembly every morning before we proceed to business, and that one or more of the clergy of this city be requested to officiate in that service.

Does that sound anti-Christian?

George Washington has also been portrayed as a "deist" or "atheist". Just look what Washington has said and done. He wrote in his prayer book: "I beseech thee, my sins, remove them from thy presence, as far as the east is from the west, and accept me for the merits of thy Son, Jesus Christ…."

In his first general order to his own troops, General Washington said he called on: "Every officer and man…to live, and act, as becomes a Christian Soldier defending the dearest rights and liberties of his country." Based on this how can one surmise that George Washington as not a Godly man? Some historians even referred to Washington as the "American Moses" who led his people from bondage to the true freedom of God.

Why is it that the three of the most famous of our Founding Fathers, George Washington, Thomas Jefferson, and Benjamin Franklin are noted by the "new historians" as un-Christian? While true history, i.e. documents and letters, show the opposite to be true.

You have read about other great leaders who are well known, such as James Madison, Samuel Adams, Patrick Henry, and Alexander Hamilton. But how many of you have even heard of Gouverneur Morris, Francis Hopkins, George Mason, Thomas McKean or Charles Carroll. These men were just as important as the likes of Jefferson, Franklin, and Hamilton. Modern history has chosen to ignore them because it would only confirm the fact that our nation was indeed founded on Judeo-Christian ideals. These were not the only founders of our nation. There are two hundred fifty more considered as "Founding Fathers" that were not mentioned here but who were just as devout as these brave Patriots.

Fifty-six signed the Declaration of Independence, fifty-five signed the Constitution of the United States of America, ninety signed the Bill of Rights, and forty-eight signed the Articles of Confederation. Sixteen signers of the Articles of Confederation also signed the Declaration of Independence. Only one person (Roger Sherman) signed all four documents.

During the 1970s and 1980s researched analyzed some fifteen thousand items of American political commentary published between 1760 and 1805, the Founding Era. They isolated 3,154 direct quotes made by the Founders and identified the source of those quotes. They discovered 34 percent of the Founding Fathers' quotes came directly out of the Bible.

While it is true that three-fourths of the biblical citations in the sample came from reprinted sermons (one of the most popular types of political writing during these years), and only 9 percent of all citations came form secular literature, it is a reflection of the powerful role of the Bible upon the thinking of the Founding Fathers.[27]

Modern history tries to ignore these Christian Patriots to further their goal of eliminating God from our country. They are doing this through our schools first, and then on to other public forums. The purpose of eliminating God is because they fear his presence and judgment for their everyday lives and lifestyles. With God looking on they can't do whatever pleases them to fulfill whatever goals they may have. The only problem with that train of thought is God **does** see! Woe unto them that turn their back on the Lord for their own selfish agenda.

As Christians, it our duty to make sure that God remains, not only a part of our lives, but a part of our nation's life. Our country is heading down a very slippery slope right now. We must do all we can to bring our country back to God almighty before it is too late.

We do not know when the end of days will come, but we do know it will come. When Jesus Christ, our Lord and Saviour, does come again, we must all be ready. We must make sure our nation greets him with open arms instead of cowering behind rocks to try to avoid the final judgment.

Woe unto them that call evil good, and good evil; that put darkness for light, and light for darkness...

–Isaiah 5:20 (KJV)

The Norwest Ordinance

On July 13, 1787, the Continental Congress passed the "Northwest Ordinance", which declared that the United States intended to settle the region north of the Ohio River and east of the Mississippi River. It set up a method by which new states would be admitted to the Union, giving them the same rights and powers as the established states, including the **freedom of religion.** It also stated the importance that Congress attached to religion: "Religion, morality, and knowledge being necessary to good government and the happiness of mankind, schools and the means of education shall forever be encouraged."

James Wilson (1742–1798), one of only six Founders to have signed both the Declaration of Independence and the Constitution, pronounced in his law lectures at the University of Pennsylvania:

"Far from being rivals or enemies, religion and law are twin sisters, friends, and mutual assistants."

Not surprisingly, throughout American history up until the middle years of the twentieth century, government looked positively on both religion and morality. Various states worked out particular arrangements reflecting their particular circumstances, but in each case, religious freedom was respected while religion was looked upon as part of the common good, a "seedbed of virtue" contributing to American society.[28]

And thou shalt teach them diligently unto thy children, and shalt talk of them when thou sittest in thine house, and when thou walkest by the way, and when thou liest down, and when thou risest up.

–Deuteronomy 6:7 (KJV)

THE SECOND "GREAT AWAKENING"

Emperor Napoleon Bonaparte had a vision of a renewed western empire for France, and his schemes included the recapture of Louisiana from Spain. Control over this vast territory would halt the westward expansion of the young United States and would supply French colonies in the West Indies with the goods they needed. In 1800, Napoleon signed the secret "Treaty of Ildefonso" with Spain. This agreement stipulated that France would provide Spain with a kingdom for the son-in-law of Spain's king if Spain would return Louisiana to France. However, Napoleon's plan collapsed when the twelve-year revolt of slaves and free blacks in the French colony of Saint-Domingue succeeded, forcing French troops to return defeated to France and preventing them from reaching their ultimate destination—Louisiana—and from being able to defend it. As Napoleon's New World Empire disintegrated, the loss of Haiti made Louisiana unnecessary.

The United States wanted to acquire the area near New Orleans primarily to guarantee its right to sail vessels down the Mississippi River through Spanish territory and unload goods at New Orleans for shipment to the Atlantic coast and Europe. Moreover, the United States wanted to possess the entire territory of Louisiana, because so many American settlers and merchants were already in the region, and because of its vital geographic position at the mouth of the Mississippi River.

The United States discovered the transfer of Louisiana from Spain to France and sent Robert Livingston to France in 1801 to try to purchase New Orleans. Napoleon initially refused, leading President Thomas Jefferson to send James Monroe to secure the deal. However, in April 1803, just days before Monroe was to arrive in Paris, Napoleon offered to sell the United States not only New Orleans but all of Louisiana. Napoleon's minister of the treasury, the Marquis de Barbé-Marbois, dealt with Livingston and Monroe over terms of the Louisiana Purchase. The United States purchased Louisiana for $11,250,000 and assumed claims of its own citizens against France up to $3,750,000, for a total purchase price of $15 million for an area of 828,800 square miles.

In order to claim its new territory with authority, the United States first had to explore and then populate it. President Jefferson commissioned Meriwether Lewis and William Clark to head the first transcontinental expedition. In May 1804, once the transfer of Louisiana to the United States was official, Lewis and Clark departed from the St. Louis area with some forty enlisted soldiers. Their journey up the Missouri River, into uncharted lands, across the Great Divide, and along the

Columbia River to the Pacific Ocean took over a year. They returned to St. Louis in September 1806.[29]

As our nation began to grow, expanding westward, the need for religious teachings also grew. A vast number of people were coming to America to take advantage of the growing economy and the new availability of land.

By the late 1700s many Americans no longer attended church services on a regular basis. Some people believed that (1) God did not play an important part in everyday life, (2) God was not concerned with a person's church attendance and (3) God would judge the person on how he or she lived his or her life here on Earth. Other people had become too consumed with earning a living to have time to worship God.

Even though times were hard for the settlers and pioneers they were risking the wrath of God by turning their backs on Him. Instead of thanking God for the land they now had and the wealth some were attaining, they ignored His blessings and chose not to worship Him according to His Law.

As a result of declining religious convictions, many religious faiths sponsored religious revivals. These revivals emphasized man's dependence upon God.

For if ye turn again unto the LORD, your brethren and your children shall find compassion... for the LORD your God is gracious and merciful, and will not turn away his face from you, if ye return unto him.

–2 Chronicles 30:9 (KJV)

Most revivals occurred as camp meetings. Interested parties would spend several days hearing the Word of God from various religious leaders. These camp meetings also served as social gatherings. Many Americans living on the frontier did not have regular contact with their neighbors. The revivals allowed these people an opportunity to hear God's Word and also provided rural families to talk and trade with other people.

This "Second Great Awakening" consisted of several kinds of activity, distinguished by locale and expression of religious commitment. In New England, the renewed interest in religion inspired a wave of social activism. In western New York, the spirit of revival encouraged the emergence of new denominations. In the Appalachian region of Kentucky and Tennessee, the revival strengthened the Methodists and the Baptists, and spawned a new form of religious expression—the camp meeting.

In contrast to the Great Awakening of the 1730s, the revivals in the East were notable for the absence of hysteria and open emotion. Rather, unbelievers were awed by the "respectful silence" of those bearing witness to their faith. The evangelical enthusiasm in New England gave rise to interdenominational missionary societies, formed to evangelize the West. Members of these societies not only acted as apostles for the faith, but as educators, civic leaders, and exponents of Eastern, urban culture. Publication and education societies promoted Christian education. Most notable among them was the American Bible Society, founded in 1816. Social activism inspired by the revival gave rise to abolition-of-slavery groups and the Society for the Promotion of Temperance, as well as to efforts to reform prisons and care for the handicapped and mentally ill.

In the Appalachian region, the revival took on characteristics similar to the Great Awakening of the previous century. But here, the center of the revival was the camp meeting, a religious service of several days' length, for a group that was obliged to take shelter on the spot because of the distance from home. Pioneers in thinly populated areas looked to the camp meeting as a refuge from the lonely life on the frontier. The sheer exhilaration of participating in a religious revival with hundreds and perhaps thousands of people inspired the dancing, shouting, and singing associated with these events. Probably the largest camp meeting was at Cane Ridge, Kentucky, in August 1801; between 10,000 and 25,000 people attended.

The great revival quickly spread throughout Kentucky, Tennessee, and southern Ohio, with the Methodists and the Baptists its prime beneficiaries. Each denomination had assets that allowed it to thrive on the frontier. The Methodists had a very efficient organization that depended on ministers—known as circuit riders—who sought out people in remote frontier locations. The circuit riders came from among the common people and possessed a rapport with the frontier families they hoped to convert. The Baptists had no formal church organization. Their farmer-preachers were people who received "the call" from God, studied the Bible, and founded a church, which then ordained them. Other candidates for the ministry emerged from these churches, and established a presence farther into the wilderness. Using such methods, the Baptists became dominant throughout the border states and most of the South.

The Second Great Awakening exercised a profound impact on American history. The numerical strength of the Baptists and Methodists rose relative to that of the denominations dominant in the Colonial period—Anglicans, Presbyterians, and Congregationalists. The growing differences within American Protestantism reflected the growth and diversity of an expanding nation."[30]

While the focus of the "Second Great Awakening" was primarily on personal salvation, it accomplished far more than that. This revival encourage Christians to become involved in causes dealing with prison reform, temperance, women's suffrage, and the movement to abolish slavery. It had a greater impact on secular society than any other than any other movement in American history.

Moreover as for me, God forbid that I should sin against the LORD in ceasing to pray for you: but I will teach you the good and the right way:
–1 Samuel 12:23 (KJV)

Charles Finney (1792–1875)

Charles Finney was one of the greatest American preachers in the 1800's. He became president of Oberlin College in Ohio. He strongly supported giving freedom to slaves, and the college was a busy station for the Underground Railroad, which secretly brought slaves to freedom. Finney also helped form a great network of volunteer societies organized to aid in solving social problems.

As preacher Finney had rare gifts. Wherever he went extensive revivals prevailed. His manner was dramatic, direct, and personal. He used simple language and illustrations. His presentation was clear and strictly logical. He directed his appeals to the conscience, rather than to the emotions, and made it tremble and quake by his searching analysis of the motives of action. He chose for themes passages which delineate the sinner's condition as one of conscious alienation from God, and sinning against him. He dwelt Upon the enmity of the carnal mind, the lack of holiness, and the certain destruction of the impenitent. He called upon his hearers to come to an immediate decision and submit to God. "Instead of telling sinners" he says, "to use the means of grace, and pray for a new heart, I called on them to make themselves a new heart and spirit, and pressed the duty of immediate surrender to God."[31]

During revivals that Finney held in Boston, fifty thousand people put their faith in Christ in just one week. Finney always demanded an answer from his question: "What will you do with Jesus Christ?" Perhaps that is what happened across America through the "Second Great Awakening". Hundreds of thousands put their faith in Christ and went on to exert a profound spiritual and social impact in their day.

And Jesus, when he came out, saw much people, and was moved with compassion toward them, because they were as sheep not having a shepherd: and he began to teach them many things.

–Mark 6:34 (KJV)

STRENGTH FOR A CHRISTIAN NATION

John Quincy Adams —6th President of the United States (1767–1848)

John Quincy Adams was the son of our 2nd President of the United States, John Adams. As the first President who was the son of a President, he in many respects paralleled the career as well as the temperament and viewpoints of his illustrious father. Adams was a Unitarian and stated his religious views on many occasions, one being on July 4th 1837 on the 61st anniversary of our independence. It was a speech delivered to the citizens of the Town of Newburyport, Massachusetts.

He quoted the Bible in various parts of his speech. He opened with:

Say ye not, A confederacy, to all them to whom this people shall say, A confederacy; neither fear ye their fear, nor be afraid.

–Isaiah 8:12 (KJV)

He went on to say:

Why is it that, next to the birthday of the Savior of the World, your most joyous and most venerated festival returns on this day? – And why is it that, among the swarming myriads of our population, thousands and tens of thousands among us, abstaining, under the dictate of religious principle, from the commemoration of that birth-day of Him, who brought life and immortality to light, yet unite with all their brethren of this community, year after year, in celebrating this, the birth-day of the nation?

Is it not that, in the chain of human events, the birthday of the nation is indissolubly linked with the birthday of the Savior? That it forms a leading event in the progress of the gospel dispensation? Is it not that the Declaration of Independence first organized the social compact on the foundation of the Redeemer's mission upon earth? That it laid the corner stone of human government upon the first precepts of Christianity, and gave to the world the first irrevocable pledge of the fulfillment of the prophecies, announced directly from Heaven at the birth of the Savior and predicted by the greatest of the Hebrew prophets six hundred years before?

...their warfare was accomplished, and the Spirit of the Lord, with a voice reaching to the latest of future ages, might have exclaimed, like the sublime prophet of Israel.

Again he quoted the Bible:

Comfort ye, comfort ye my people, saith your God.

–Isaiah 40:1 (KJV)

...In the common intercourse of social life, the birth-day of individuals is often held as a yearly festive day by themselves, and their immediate relatives; yet, as early as the age of Solomon, that wisest of men told the people of Jerusalem:

A good name is better than precious ointment; and the day of death than the day of one's birth.

–Ecclesiastes 7:1 (KJV)

To show the devotion to the Bible Adams also stated:

At this day, religious indulgence is one of our clearest duties, because it is one of our undisputed rights. While we rejoice that the principles of genuine Christianity have so far triumphed over the prejudices of a former generation, let us fervently hope for the day when it will prove equally victorious over the malignant passions of our own. –Oration at Plymouth, 22 December 1802

The neglect of public worship in this city is an increasing evil, and the indifference to all religion throughout the whole country portends no good. There is in the clergy of all the Christian denominations a time-serving, cringing, subservient morality, as wide from the spirit of the Gospel as it is from the intrepid assertion and vindication of truth. The counterfeit character of a very large portion of the Christian ministry of this country is disclosed in the dissensions growing up in all the Protestant churches on the subject of slavery. The abolitionists assume as the first principle of all their movements that slavery is sin. Their opponents, halting between the alternative of denying directly this position and of admitting the duty binding upon them to bear their own testimony against it, are prevaricating with their own consciences, and taxing their learning and ingenuity to prove that the Bible sanctions slavery; that Abraham, Isaac, and Paul were slave-holders; and that St. Paul is the apostle of man-stealers, because he sent Onesimus back to his master Philemon. These preachers of the Gospel might just as well call our extermination of the Indians obedience to Divine commands because Jehovah commanded the children of Israel to exterminate the Canaanitish nations. –Diary, 27 May 1838

John Quincy Adams' father John Adams was one of the most religious of the Founding Fathers. He taught his son well in the Bible as well as in politics. John Quincy Adams followed his father in leading this nation with his biblical views and devotion to Christ.

Rooted and built up in him, and established in the faith, as ye have been taught, abounding therein with thanksgiving.

–Colossians 2:7 (KJV)

Andrew Jackson—7th President of the United States (1767–1845)

The conversion of Andrew Jackson

The following is an excerpt from "What had God Wrought! –A biblical interpretation of American History" by William P. Grady[32] (permission granted)

The Battle of New Orleans had made Andrew Jackson a national hero overnight. But mere early accomplishments can never fill the void that exists in a lost man's soul. Besides, the humble general had more sense than the editors of Laissez Faire Books concerning the ultimate cause for his victory, acknowledging to a friend, "It appears that the unerring hand of Providence shielded my men from the shower of balls, bombs, and rockets, when every ball and bomb from our guns carried with them a mission of death."

Andrew Jackson was better known for his attendance at duels than at church, but on a particular Monday in October of 1818, he decided to visit a revival service in Nashville where the controversial Peter Cartwright was scheduled to speak. As it happened, the General entered as the preacher was reading his text, "For what shall it profit a man, if he shall gain the whole world, and lose his own soul?" (Mark 8:36) With all the seats already occupied, the famous Indian fighter and war hero was content to stand, gracefully leaning on the middle post. At the sight of his stately appearance, the host pastor, a certain "Brother Mac," became nervous in the extreme. Seated on the platform directly behind the pulpit, he tugged on Cartwright's jacket, whispering, "General Jackson has come in; General Jackson has come in." Cartwright was aghast at the pastor's double standard:

"I felt a flash of indignation run all over me like an electric shock, and facing about to my congregation, and purposely speaking out audibly, I said, "Who is General Jackson? If he don't get his soul converted, God will damn him as quick as he would a Guinea negro." The preacher tucked his head down, and squatted low, and would, no doubt, have been thankful for leave of absence. The congregation, General Jackson and all smiled or laughed right out, all at the preacher's expense.

When the congregation was dismissed, my city-stationed preacher stepped up to me and very sternly said to me: "You are the strangest man I ever saw, and General Jackson will chastise you for your insolence before you leave the city." "Very clear of it," said I, "for General Jackson, I have no doubt, will applaud my course; and if he should undertake to chastise me…there is two as can play that game."

"Next morning, very early, my city preacher went down to the hotel to make an apology to General Jackson for my conduct in the pulpit the night before. Shortly after he had left I passed by the hotel and I met the General on the pavement; and before I approached him by several steps he smiled, and reached out his hand and said: "Mr. Cartwright, you are a man after my own heart. I am very surprised at Mr. Mac, to think that I would be offended at you. No, sir; I told him that I highly approved of your independence; that a minister of Jesus Christ ought to love every body and fear no mortal man. I told Mr. Mac that if I had a few thousand such independent, fearless officers as you were, and a well drilled army, I could take Old England."

Acknowledging that Jackson was "no doubt in his prime of life, a very wicked man," Cartwright relates the following story to illustrate the General's "great respect for the Christian religion, and the feelings of religious people, especially ministers of the Gospel":

"I had preached one Sabbath near the Hermitage, and, in company with several gentlemen and ladies, went, by special invitation, to dine with the General. Among this company there was a young sprig of a lawyer from Nashville, of very ordinary intellect, and he was trying hard to make an infidel of himself. As I was the only preacher present, this young lawyer kept pushing his conversation on me, in order to get into an argument. I tried to evade an argument, in the first place considering it a breach of good manners to interrupt the social conversation of the company. In the second place I plainly saw that his head was much softer than his heart and that there were no laurels to be won by vanquishing or demolishing such a combatant and I persisted in evading an argument.

"This seemed to inspire the young man with more confidence in himself; for my evasiveness he construed into fear. I saw General Jackson's eye strike fire, as he sat by and heard the thrusts he made at the Christian religion. At length the young lawyer asked me this question: "Mr. Cartwright, do you really believe there is any such place as hell, as a place of torment?" I answered promptly, "Yes, I do." To which he responded, "Well, I thank God I have too much good sense to believe any such thing."

"I was pondering in my mind whether I would answer him or not, when General Jackson for the first time broke into the conversation, and directing his words to the young man, said with great earnestness: "Well, sir, I thank God that there is such a place of torment as hell." This sudden answer, made with great earnestness, seemed to astonish the youngster, and he exclaimed: "Why, General Jackson, what do you want with such a place of torment as hell?" To which the General replied, as quick as lightning, "To put such [expletive] rascals as you are in, that oppose and vilify the Christian religion."

It was about this same time (1818) that Jackson invaded the Spanish held territory of eastern Florida in order to stop frontier attacks by the Seminole Indians. He eventually defeated the Seminoles, drove out the Spanish and seized control of Florida. By the year 1828, Andrew Jackson was the undisputed people's choice for president. A contemporary of the new chief executive wrote, "History is sure to preserve the name of any man who has had the strength and genius to stamp his own character on the people over whose destinies he presided."

However, Jackson's greatest triumph came on the eve of his greatest personal tragedy. Before the new president could be sworn into office, his beloved wife succumbed to a massive heart attack. On Christmas Eve, 1828, Rachel was laid to rest in her garden. A friend of the widower related, "I never pitied any person more in my life... I shall never forget his look of grief."

Jackson had many enemies in the banking industry because of his incessant attacks on the nation's third central bank, called the Second Bank of the United States (a battle he would eventually win). In January of 1835, a bearded man attempted to assassinate the President, firing two pistols at him at point-blank range. For some reason, both guns failed to discharge. Having received a letter of concern from the King of England, Jackson wrote back exclaiming, "A kind of Providence had been pleased to shield me against the recent attempt upon my life, and irresistibly carried many minds to the belief in a superintending Providence."

On March 4, 1837, President Jackson delivered his Farewell Address and reiterated the theme of America's unique destiny in world history:

You have the highest of human trusts committed to your care. Providence has showered on this favored land blessings without number, and has chosen you as the guardians of freedom, to preserve it for the benefit of the human race. May He who holds in His hands the destinies of nations, make you worthy of the favors He has bestowed, and enable you, with pure hearts and hands and sleepless vigilance, to guard and defend to the end of time, the great charge He has committed to your keeping.

Retirement years brought on seasons of serious reflection. The seed sown by Peter Cartwright was finally ready to bear fruit as God's Word was not about to return void. Chamberlain writes:

The evening of his stormy life had come. The remains of his much loved wife were resting in the humble graveyard near the house. At last thoughts of eternity were forced upon him. After attending a series of religious meetings Jackson became greatly convicted of his sin. He passed the night walking in his chamber in anguish and prayer. In the morning he announced to his family his full conviction that he had repented of his sins, and, through faith in Jesus Christ, had obtained forgiveness. Family prayer was immediately established... he was privileged to read through the Bible twice.

On May 29, 1845, only a few weeks before his death, Jackson declared:

Sir, I am in the hands of a merciful God. I have full confidence in his goodness and mercy... The Bible is true... Upon that sacred volume I rest my hope for eternal salvation, through the merits and blood of our blessed Lord and Saviour, Jesus Christ.

Finally, on June 8, 1845, just moments before he sailed into eternity, Jackson reassured everyone with these words:

My dear children, do not grieve for me; it is true, I am going to leave you; I am well aware of my situation. I have suffered much bodily pain, but my sufferings are as nothing compared with that which our blessed Redeemer endured upon the accursed Cross, that all might be saved who put their trust in Him... God will take care of you for me. I am my God's. I belong to Him. I go but a short time before you, and... I hope and trust to meet you all in Heaven, both white and black.

Before expiring, Andrew Jackson made a last appeal for America to build her future on the blessed Word of God. "That book, Sir, is the Rock upon which our republic rests."

For what shall it profit a man, if he shall gain the whole world, and lose his own soul?

–Mark 8:36 (KJV)

Alexis De Tocqueville (1805–1859)

In 1831, Alexis De Tocqueville, a young French nobleman, spent nine months traveling America. He interviewed people from every walk of life, then wrote down some amazing observations in "Democracy in America". He wrote:

Upon my arrival in the United States, the religious aspects of the country was the first thing that struck my attention...I perceived the great political consequences resulting from this state of things...

In France I had almost always seen the spirit of religion and the spirit of freedom pursuing courses diametrically opposed to each other; but in America I found that they were intimately united, and that they reigned in common over the same country.

...there is no country in the whole world in which the Christian religion retains a greater influence over the souls of men than in America; and there can be no greater proof of it utility, and of its conformity to human nature, than that its influence is most powerfully felt over the most enlightened and free nation of the earth.

Religion in America takes no direct part in the government of society, but it must nevertheless be regarded as the foremost of the political institutions of that country...This opinion is not peculiar to a class of citizens or to a party, but it belongs to the whole nation, and to every rank of society.

The Americans combine the notions of Christianity and of liberty so intimately in their minds, that it is impossible to conceive the one without the other."[33]

But whoso looketh into the perfect law of liberty, and continueth therein, he being not a forgetful hearer, but a doer of the work, this man shall be blessed in his deed.

–James 1:25 (KJV)

Daniel Webster (1782–1852)

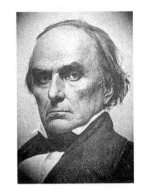

Daniel Webster was a leading American statesman and considered one of the greatest orators in American history. He served as a U.S. congressman, senator, and as the Secretary of State for three different presidents. In a speech given before the Historical Society of New York, February 23, 1852, he said:

> If we and our posterity shall be true to the Christian religion, if we and they shall live always in the fear of God, and shall respect His commandments, if we and they shall maintain just moral sentiments and such conscientious convictions of duty as shall control the heart and life, we may have the highest hopes of the future fortunes of our country; and if we maintain those institutions of government and that political union, exceeding all praise as much as it exceeds all former examples of political associations, we may be sure of one thing...It will have no decline and fall. It will go on prospering and to prosper.
>
> But if we and our posterity reject religious institutions and authority, violate the rules of eternal justice, trifle with the injunctions of morality, and recklessly destroy the political constitution which holds us together, no man can tell how sudden a catastrophe may overwhelm us that shall bury all our glory in profound obscurity.[34]

Daniel Webster also said: "God grants liberty only to those who love it and are always ready to guard and defend it."

Beloved, I wish above all things that thou mayest prosper and be in health, even as thy soul prospereth.

–3 John 1:2 (KJV)

Mr. Webster was right. Our nation as a whole has rejected the religious institutions and authority, and look what is happening in our country now. We are in the worse moral decline of our history, we are in the worst economic climate we have seen in generations, and we are no longer considered the moral leader of the world. Our leaders are turning their backs not only on our own history and principles of our Founding Fathers but also on God. If we are to continue on this path, there is only one possible outcome. The abandonment of God, and his eternal Blessings.

THE CIVIL WAR

While the reasons for the Revolutionary War are very clear, the reasons for the Civil War are still being debated today. Political disagreements between the North and South began soon after the American Revolution ended in 1782, and those arguments mounted between 1800 and 1860. Disputes over unfair taxes paid on goods brought into the South from foreign countries as well as perceived shifts of political power in the federal government to favor the North and Midwestern states fueled the Southern call away from the central federal authority in Washington and to a restoration of states' rights.

Religion and the Bible were so entrenched in the hearts and minds of the American people that after the Confederate forces fired upon Fort Sumter in April 1861 that the vast majority of Northern religious bodies passionately supported the war for the Union. Protestants enjoyed a significant numerical and cultural dominance in the 1860s and contributed to the religious justifications of the war and had a wider social and political impact.

The churches emphasized that the Union had to be preserved because of the special place that America had in world history. With its republican institutions, democratic ideals, and Christian values, the United States stood in the forefront of civilization's march to the future. So in fighting to save the Union, Northerners were struggling on behalf of more than a single nation, they were fighting for the future of humanity itself.

However, slavery was the defining issue that drove Southern resolve to make war on the Union rather than accept Abraham Lincoln's election as President in 1860. In the early 1800s slavery was first seen as an economic issue and second as a moral issue. Extensive theological debate was waged over the biblical understanding of slavery, which Scripture never expressly denounces. Abolitionists gave convincing argument that the spirit of the Bible condemned slavery. But the bottom line was that if the South lost her slaves, her socio-economic system would collapse.

The South believed that the North was threatening their way of life, that it was their sovereign right to secede from the Union, and that the institution of slavery was ordained by God and upheld in the Bible.

Each side believed emphatically that God was on its side in the conflict. From early Colonial days, New England political and religious leaders had considered themselves as God's "chosen people." With the start of the Civil War Southerners invoked "the favor and guidance of Almighty God" in their constitution, proclaiming themselves a Christian nation. Ministers, generals, political leaders, and newspaper editors went so far as to claim the God had ordained the war and was sovereign to determine all its outcomes.

The sense that God was decisively at work in the war between the states also greatly altered the way in which church leaders viewed slavery. At the beginning of the war Northern churches were not unanimous in their attitude toward slavery. A few denounced the practice as a sin and called for immediate emancipation and abolition. The other extreme argued that the Bible treated slavery as a morally legitimate institution. For example parts of the Old Testament law recognized and regulated slavery. Jesus lived in a culture of slavery and apparently said nothing against it. The letters of the apostle Paul contained explicit commands that slaves be obedient to their masters.

Servants, be obedient to them that are your masters...
–Ephesians 6:5 (KJV)

Most church leaders appear to have fallen somewhere between these extremes. They considered slavery less than ideal and believed it would eventually be eradicated by slow and peaceful means. Proslavery and abolitionist alike were prepared to await God's resolution of the matter.

At the start of the war the Northern position was to save the Union not to free the slaves. Mixed results on the battlefield prompted a reassessment of their goals. In Virginia the Union army had a succession of defeats. Believing that the hand of God was in every event, Protestant ministers sought a theological explanation for military failure.

They drew on a tradition traceable to Puritan preaching – the jeremiad – to explain the reverses. The jeremiad was a sermon form (named after the Old

Testament prophet Jeremiah) that threatened people with judgment unless they renounced their sins; or alternately the jeremiad took some current disaster, interpreted it as a punishment sent by God, and then asked for what sin the penalty had been imposed. The defeat of Union armies seemed to be punishment of this sort, and the conviction grew that God would continue to chastise the North and would not allow it to win the war until it took steps to end slavery...religious groups concluded that the war had signaled God's intention that slavery die and die NOW.[35]

Abraham Lincoln—16th President of the United States (1809–1865)

On March 3, 1863, the U.S. Senate passed a resolution asking President Abraham Lincoln to designate a day "for national prayer and humiliation," stating that the Senate was "devoutly recognizing the supreme authority and just government of Almighty God in all the affairs of men and of nations, and sincerely believing that no people can prosper without His favor," and encouraged by "His word to seek Him for succor according to His appointed way, through Jesus Christ."

In response to a U.S. Senate resolution, President Abraham Lincoln issued a proclamation designating April 30, 1863, as a day of "national humiliation, fasting and prayer," stating that:

> ...it is the duty of nations as well as of men to own their dependence upon the overruling power of God, to confess their sins and transgressions in humble sorrow, yet with assured hope that genuine repentance will lead to mercy and pardon, and to recognize the sublime truth, announced in the Holy Scriptures and proven by all history, *that those nations only are blessed whose God is the Lord*.

In Abraham Lincoln's Second Inaugural Address of March 1865 he said:

> Both the North and South read the same Bible, and pray to the same God; and each invokes His aid against the other. It may seem strange that any men should dare to ask a just God's assistance in wringing their bread from the sweat of the other men's faces; but let us judge not that

we be not judged. The prayers of both could not be answered; that of neither has been answered fully. The Almighty has His own purposes.

In 1864 Joshua Speed, a close friend of Lincoln's, was visiting him and came upon him reading his Bible. Lincoln said to him:

...Take all of this book upon reason that you can, and the balance on faith, and you will live and die a happier and better man.:

But let him ask in faith, nothing wavering. For he that wavereth is like a wave of the sea driven with the wind and tossed.
–James 1:6 (KJV)

As America entered the dark days of the Civil War, President Abraham Lincoln realized the need for the nation to turn its heart to God. After the Union Army's defeat at the Battle of Bull Run, President Lincoln called the American people to a time of repentance, prayer, and fasting, so that "the united prayer of the nation may ascend to the throne of grace and bring down plentiful blessings upon our country."

Other Quotations by Abraham Lincoln:

"God must love the common man, he made so many of them."

"Sir, my concern is not whether God is on our side; my greatest concern is to be on God's side, for God is always right."

"Surely God would not have created such a being as man, with an ability to grasp the infinite, to exist only for a day! No, no, man was made for immortality."

"In great contests each party claims to act in accordance with the will of God. Both may be, and one must be wrong."

As you can see even during times of great conflict, the people of the United States and their leaders were deeply religious; always looking for guidance from Almighty God. Whether or not they were on the right side of the conflict, they thought God was on their side. They prayed for guidance and deliverance for their goals.

In the Bible, the book of "First Kings" records the life and reign of Israel's King Solomon, considered the wisest man who ever lived. When Solomon heeded God's Word and followed the directives handed down through his father King David, Israel enjoyed unprecedented peace, prosperity, and blessing. But when, toward the end of his life, Solomon took his eyes off the God-inspired vision for Israel, the nation began a slow decline.

Similarly, the far-reaching vision that led America's forefathers to found a nation governed by the rule of law, could not prevent that nation from splintering less than eighty years later as self-centered ideologies and a militant spirit threatened to destroy this "one nation under God." Only God's mercy, righteous leadership, and prayers of individuals and groups who love their God and their country, have helped keep America as the "land of the free and the home of the brave."[36]

We are currently experiencing a rapid decline in our moral and national values due to the immoral leadership of our country. We must get back to the Lord our God in order to keep our country from the total decline experienced by godless countries such a those in Eastern Europe and Asia.

It is only through God's mercy and the prayers of the Christians of this nation that we are still thriving in the way we are. However, if we continue on the path of self-destruction through ignoring God's Word and Law we are doomed to oblivion.

The LORD shall send upon thee cursing, vexation, and rebuke, in all that thou settest thine hand unto for to do, until thou be destroyed, and until thou perish quickly; because of the wickedness of thy doings, whereby thou hast forsaken me.

–Deuteronomy 28:20 (KJV)

Chapter Two

LEADING A
CHRISTIAN NATION

After the Civil War ended our nation continued to grow both economically and spiritually. Many of our presidents, supreme court justices, and others leaders of this great nation were very religious and adhered to the Judeo-Christian beliefs of our Founding Fathers as evidenced by their personal and professional writings and speeches.

James Garfield—20th President of the United States (1831–1881)

James A. Garfield was an attorney, minister, educator, soldier, and the twentieth President of the United States. He experienced a dramatic conversion to Christianity in his youth while working on the Ohio canal and was later licensed as a minister in the Christian Church; member of the U. S. House of Representatives (1863-80); elected President of the United States (1880).

As the last of the log cabin Presidents, James A. Garfield attacked political corruption and won back for the Presidency a measure of prestige it had lost during the Reconstruction period.

On July 2, 1881, in a Washington railroad station, an embittered attorney who had sought a consular post shot the President.

Mortally wounded, Garfield lay in the White House for weeks. Alexander Graham Bell, inventor of the telephone, tried unsuccessfully to find the bullet with an induction-balance electrical device which he had designed. On September 6, Garfield was taken to the New Jersey seaside. For a few days he seemed to be recuperating, but on September 19, 1881, he died from an infection and internal hemorrhage.

Before being elected President of the United States, James Garfield was a minister of "Christian Church (Disciples of Christ)." In 1858 he preached at 19 revivals and baptized 31 new converts to Christ.

Garfield recounts the results of a revival he just preached in this 1858 letter:

Hiram, Feb. 16th 1858
Dear Bro. Wallace

We have just closed our meeting with happy results. There were 34 additions[s]. 31 by immersion. I was sorry I could not be in Newburgh last Sunday, but it seemed to be my duty to stay here. Bro Dave Shu[?] tells me that the Brethren want me to hold a meeting in vacation. I have spoken 19 discourses in our meeting here—and this with all our work in the school has worn me down very much. I would not think of holding a meeting alone. And don't know as I ought to help hold one. I will be in your place sometime next week and talk with you in reference to the matter of your letter. Which would have been answered sooner but for the meeting. I shall hope to visit Bedford also. Love to your family & believe me your brother,

J. A. Garfield[37]

When Garfield was inaugurated as President of the United States on March 4, 1881, he put placed his hand on the Bible on **Proverbs 21:1**;

The king's heart is in the hand of the LORD, like the rivers of water; He turns it wherever He wishes. (KJV)

James Garfield also wrote:

The world's history is a Divine poem, of which the history of every nation is a canto and every man a word. Its strains have been pealing along down the centuries, and though there have been mingled the discords of warring cannons and dying men, yet to the Christian philosopher and historian—the humble listener—there has been a Divine melody running through the song which speaks of hope and halcyon days to come.

And I will shake all nations, and the desire of all nations shall come: and I will fill this house with glory, saith the LORD of hosts.

–Haggai 2:7 (KJV)[38]

Supreme Court Justice David Josiah Brewer (1837–1910)

In 1892, the United States Supreme Court determined, in the case *The Church of the Holy Trinity vs. United States,* that an English minister was not a foreign laborer under the U.S. Code statute even though he was a foreigner. While this case was not specifically about religion and considered the legality of contracts for other foreign professionals, the court considered America's Christian identity to be a strong support for its conclusion that Congress could not have intended to prohibit ministers.

Justice Brewer penned the court's opinion, in which he stated that the United States was a "Christian nation." The Court had already decided the issue before venturing its opinion as to the religious character of the country. Included was a remarkable list of 87 examples taken from pre-Constitutional documents, historical practice, Colonial charters, and the like, which reveal our undisputed religious roots. They range from the commission of Christopher Columbus to the first charter of Virginia to the Declaration of Independence and included the following statements:

No purpose of action against religion can be imputed to any legislation, state or national, because this is a religious people...From the discovery of this continent to the present hour, there is a single voice making affirmation...There is a universal language pervading them all, having one meaning; they affirm and reaffirm that this is a religious nation. These are not individual sayings, declarations of private persons: they are organic utterances; they speak the voice of the entire people... These, and many other matters which might be noticed, add a volume of unofficial declarations to the mass of organic utterances that this is a Christian nation.

Justice Brewer later clarified his position on a "Christian nation," stating the United States is "Christian" in that many of its traditions are rooted in Christianity, not that Christianity should receive legal privileges or is established to the exclusion of other religions or to the exclusion of irreligion.[39]

He truly believed that a Christian nation was a strong nation. As long as we remained a Christian nation we would be protected by God almighty and thus would prosper.

...We have a strong city; salvation will God appoint for walls and bulwarks. Open ye the gates, that the righteous nation which keepeth the truth may enter in.

–Isaiah 26:1-2 (KJV)

Supreme Court Justice Joseph Story (1779–1845)

At the age of thirty-two Joseph became the youngest Associate Justice of the Supreme Court and served from 1811 to 1845, writing 286 opinions. He also wrote many legal texts now considered classics.

At one point in his life Story doubted the truth of Christianity. He *"labored and read with assiduous attention all of the arguments of its proof"* and became committed to the principles of Christianity, which he repeatedly expressed throughout his legal career. It was his conviction that American law and legal practices must never be separated from Christian principles.

He stated:

One of the beautiful boasts of our municipal jurisprudence is that Christianity is a part of the Common Law...There has never been a period in which the Common Law did not recognize Christianity as lying at it foundations...The law pronounces illegal every contract offensive to Christianity's morals. It recognizes with profound humility Christianity's holidays and festivals, and obeys them even to the point of suspending all government functions on those days. It still attaches to persons believing in Christianity's divine authority the highest degree of competency as witnesses.[40]

In 1844, a school run by the city of Philadelphia adopted a policy of prohibiting Christian ministers from teaching in a public school. That school operated on the philosophy that students could successfully learn morality apart from Christianity or the Bible. This philosophy is embraced by many school districts today.

Perceived as an attempt to keep the Bible from students, this policy became an issue before the United States Supreme Court. The Court's ruling was unanimous and was delivered by Justice Joseph Story. In that decision the Court declared:

Why may not the Bible, and especially the New Testament...be read and taught as a divine revelation in the school—its general precepts expounded...and its glorious principles of morality inculcated? ...Where can the purest principles of morality be learned as clearly or so perfectly as from the New Testament.[41]

The United States Supreme Court unanimously held that this government-run school should teach Christianity and the Bible. Modern rulings are exactly the opposite, but few today realize that earlier Courts—Courts whose Justices were appointed by Founding Fathers—have already addressed the same issues.[42]

In 1811 New York Supreme Court—a ruling subsequently cited by the U.S. Supreme Court as an authority for its own decisions. That New York case dealt with a man who had distributed writing full of vulgar, malicious, and gratuitous profanity, attacking God, Jesus Christ, and the Bible. He was fined and punished, and on appeal the state supreme court upheld the conviction, stressing that, "Whatever strikes at the root of Christianity tends manifestly to the dissolution of civil government."[43]

The Founding Fathers purposely appointed Christian, Bible believing men to the Supreme Court, believing that there actions would be guided by God, and that their decisions would be based on moral and biblical interpretations. This, in their opinion, would keep the nation strong and prosperous.

And when the LORD raised them up judges, then the LORD was with the judge, and delivered them out of the hand of their enemies all the days of the judge...

–Judges 2:18 (KJV)

The "Separation of Church and State", as we know it today, was not the intention of the Founding Fathers. It is the exact opposite. It was fully understood by the Founding Fathers that the First Amendment was to protect rather than prevent public religious expressions. As a matter of fact the phrase "separation of church and state" does not even appear in the First Amendment at all.

The term "separation of church and state" came from Thomas Jefferson in a letter to the Danbury Baptists on January 1, 1802. He was assuring them that their free exercise of religion was indeed an inalienable right and would not be meddled with by the government. There was a "wall of separation between church and state" that would prevent the government from interfering with or hindering religious activities.

In 1853 (half a century after Jefferson wrote that phrase) a group petitioned Congress, urging them to separate Christian principles from government, with chaplains being turned out of Congress and the military, and Christian principles being removed from government and the official public squares. They wanted the government, instead of protecting religious expression in the public arena, to remove them.

Congress examined the possibility and then emphatically rejected it, declaring:

Had the people during the Revolution had a suspicion of any attempt to war against Christianity, that the Revolution would have been strangled in its cradle. At the time of the adoption of the Constitution and the amendments, the universal sentiment was that Christianity should be encouraged, but not any one denomination...In this age, there is no substitute for Christianity...That was the religion of the founders of the republic and they expressed it to remain the religion of their descendants.

In short, Congress affirmed that the First Amendment had never been intended to secularize the public square but just the opposite. In fact two years later, Congress reiterated "The great, vital, and conservative element in our system is the belief of our people in the pure doctrines and divine truths of the Gospel of Jesus Christ."[44]

Booker T. Washington (1856–1915)

Booker T. Washington was the most influential American black leader and educator of his time. He was founder and head of the Tuskegee Institute, a vocational school for blacks in Tuskegee, Alabama. He also advised two Presidents—Theodore Roosevelt and William Howard Taft—on racial issues and policies.

Washington insisted on high moral character for both students and faculty. His clear emphasis on the value of character and the training of the "head, hand, and heart" was filled with great insight. Christian faith was something Washington learned in Sunday school. At Tuskegee Institute devotional exercises were held every morning as well as evening prayers. He wrote that the support that *"the Christ-like work which the Church of all denominations in America has done"* would have convinced him of the value of the Christian life, if he wasn't already a believer.[45]

> *Then I told them of the hand of my God which was good upon me; as also the king's words that he had spoken unto me. And they said, Let us rise up and build. So they strengthened their hands for this good work.*
> *–Nehemiah 2:18 (KJV)*

Zachary Taylor 12th President of the United States (1784 –1850)

Taylor was elected president in 1848 after a 40-year career in the military. At the age of 64 when elected, he is among the oldest to serve as president. (In the 20th century, only Ronald Reagan and George H.W. Bush were older when they came to office.) Taylor fought in the War of 1812, the Black Hawk War, the Seminole War—where he earned his nickname "Old Rough and Ready" due to his preference for rumpled clothes and straw hat, rather than a uniform—and the Mexican War.

President Taylor was not one of our most religious presidents, but when Inauguration Day fell on Sunday, March 4, 1849. Taylor and his vice president Millard Fillmore both refused to be sworn in on a Sunday, so the ceremony was postponed a day. While neither Taylor nor Fillmore were outwardly religious they both sought to honor the tradition and biblical teachings about the Sabbath.

Remember the Sabbath day, to keep it holy.

–Exodus 20:8 (KJV)

And he said unto them, The Sabbath was made for man, and not man for the Sabbath:

–Mark 2:27 (KJV)

Rutherford B. Hayes 19th President of the United States (1822–1893)

Rutherford Birchard Hayes was elected in 1877 by only one electoral vote. He however lost the popular vote. His was the only presidency that was decided by a congressional commission. There were disputes over the results in South Carolina, Louisiana, Florida and one vote in Oregon. Although Hayes told a reporter that he thought he had lost the election, his party refused to concede defeat. After much controversy, Congress appointed a committee to sort out the mess. Eight  Republicans and seven Democrats sat on it, and each voted on party lines, allowing Hayes to clinch victory by 185 electoral votes to 184.

Hayes felt uncomfortable about how he won the election and vowed to only remain for just one term. He is considered my many to be the most honest and decent man to ever occupy the White House.

In his Inaugural Address Rutherford Hayes stated:

Looking for the guidance of the Divine Hand by which the destinies of nations and individuals are shaped, I call upon you, Senators, Representatives, judges, fellow citizens, here and everywhere, to unite with me in a earnest effort to secure to our country the blessings, not only of material property, but of justice, peace, and union; a union depending not upon the constraint of force but upon the loving devotion of a free people; and that all things may be so ordered and settled upon the best and surest foundations that peace and happiness, truth and justice, religion and piety, may be established among us for all generations.

Fulfilling the spirit of his inaugural address, Hayes ended reconstruction and removed all federal troops from the South. He also put the country back on the Gold Standard, reformed the civil service and suppressed the railroad strikes.

Hayes considered himself to be a Christian. Many of his writings reflect this, including the following quotations from his Diary:

...The great abyss, the unknown future, — are we not happier if we give ourselves up to some settled faith? Can we feel safe without it? Am I not more and more carried along, drifted, towards surrendering to the best religion the world has yet produced? It seems so. In this business, as I ride through the glorious scenery this loveliest season of the year, my thoughts float away beyond this wretched war and all its belongings. Some, yes many, glorious things, as well as all that is not so, [impress me]; and [I] think of the closing years on the down-hill side of life, and picture myself a Christian, sincere, humble, devoted, as conscientious in that as I am now in this—not more so. My belief in this war is as deep as any faith can be;—but thitherward I drift. I see it and am glad. –Diary, 29 October 1861

Our County Bible Society holds its yearly meeting soon. As one of the vice-presidents of the general society of the county, as a non-church member, a non-professor of religion, I may say why men of the world, friends of their country and of their race, should support the religion of the Bible—the Christian religion. To worship—'the great Creator to adore'—the wish to establish relations with the Omnipotent Power which made the universe, and which controls it, is a deeply seated principle of human nature. It is found among all races of men. It is well-nigh universal. All peoples have some religion. In our day men who cast off the Christian religion show the innate tendency by spending time and effort in Spiritualism. If the God of the Bible is dethroned the goddess of reason is set up. Religion always has been, always will be. Now, the best religion the world has ever had is the religion of Christ. A man or a community adopting it is virtuous, prosperous, and happy...

What a great mistake the man makes who goes about to oppose this religion! What a crime, if we may judge of men's acts by their results! Nay, what a great mistake is made by him who does not support the religion of the Bible! –Diary, 15 October 1884

I am not a subscriber to any creed. I belong to no church. But in a sense, satisfactory to myself and believed by me to be important, I try to be a Christian, or rather I want to be a Christian and to help do Christian work. –Diary, May 17, 1890

I am a Christian according to my conscience in belief, not of course in character and conduct, but in purpose and wish;—not of course by the orthodox standard. But I am content, and have a feeling of trust and safety. –Diary, 8 January 1893[46]

Wouldn't this be a better nation and a better world if we all had the same belief and passion as that of Rutherford B. Hayes? Even though he was not a "practicing Christian", he was a Christian in heart. We should all learn a lesson from Mr. Hayes. We should learn that the one and only true religion is the religion of Jesus Christ. Only Jesus Christ can keep us from harm in our personal lives, as well as our national survival. Always look to God for the answers, He will light your way.

For the commandment is a lamp; and the law is light; and reproofs of instruction are the way of life:

–Proverbs 6:23 (KJV)

Theodore Roosevelt 26th President of the United States (1858–1919)

With the assassination of President McKinley, Theodore Roosevelt, not quite 43, became the youngest President in the Nation's history. He brought new excitement and power to the Presidency, as he vigorously led Congress and the American public toward progressive reforms and a strong foreign policy.

He took the view that the President as a "steward of the people" should take whatever action necessary for the public good unless expressly forbidden by law or the

Constitution." I did not usurp power," he wrote, "but I did greatly broaden the use of executive power."

Roosevelt steered the United States more actively into world politics. He liked to quote a favorite proverb, *"Speak softly and carry a big stick…"*[7]

When he took the presidential oath of office he place his hand on James 1:22, 23:

But be ye doers of the word, and not hearers only, deceiving your own selves. For if any be a hearer of the word, and not a doer, he is like unto a man beholding his natural face in a glass:

–James 1:22-23 (KJV)

Theodore Roosevelt is considered by many historians to be one of the greatest U.S. presidents. He also had a very thorough knowledge of the Bible.

Every thinking man, when he thinks, realizes that the teachings of the Bible are so interwoven and entwined with our whole civic and social life that it would be literally impossible for us to figure ourselves what that life would be if these standards were removed. We would lose almost all the standards by which we now judge both public and private morals, all the standards which we, with more or less resolution, strive to raise ourselves.

Theodore Roosevelt's published works were found to contain over 4,200 Biblical images, inferences, and quotations. His unpublished letters contained thousands more.[48]

In 1917, when American troops were preparing to sail across the seas in order to take to the battlefields of France and Belgium in the first World War, the New York Bible Society asked Roosevelt to inscribe a message in the pocket New Testament that each of the soldiers would be given. The great man happily complied. And he began by giving a striking Biblical call for a life of balance, what he called *"Micah mandate:"*

He has shown you, O man, what is good; And what does the Lord require of you But to do justly, To love mercy ,And to walk humbly with your God?

–Micah 6:8

Saying that the whole teaching of the New Testament is actually foreshadowed in Micah's verse, he exhorted the men to "lead the world in both word and deed through unimpeachable moral uprightness."

In his brief message to the soldiers he explained:

Do justice, and therefore fight valiantly against those that stand for the reign of Moloch and Beelzebub on this Earth. Love mercy, treat your enemies well, succor the afflicted, treat every women as if she were your sister, care for the little children, and be tender with the old and helpless. Walk humbly, you will do so if you study the life and teachings of the Saviour, walking in His steps.

Other quotes from Roosevelt are:

A thorough knowledge of the Bible is worth more than a college education.

The eighth commandment says, 'Thou shalt not steal.' It does not say 'Thou shalt not steal from the rich,' and it does not say 'Thou shalt not steal from the poor man.' It reads simply and plainly 'Thou shalt not steal.

Fear God in the true sense of the word means to love God, respect God, honor God, and all of this can only be done by loving your neighbor, treating him justly and mercifully and in all ways endeavoring to protect him from injustice and cruelty, thus obeying, as far as our human frailty will permit, the great immutable law of righteousness.

It does so rest my soul to come into the house of the Lord and worship, and to sing and to mean it, the Holy, Holy, Holy, Lord God Almighty, and to know that He is my Father and takes me up in His life and plans, and to commune personally with Christ. I am sure I get a wisdom not my own, and superhuman strength, for fighting the moral evils I am called to confront.

On Sunday, go to church. Yes, I know all the excuses. I know that one can worship the Creator and dedicate oneself to good living in a grove of trees, or by a running brook, or in one's own house, just as well as in

Church. "But I also know as a matter of cold fact that the average man does not thus worship or thus himself. If he stays away from Church, he does not spend his time in good works or lofty meditation.

He looks over the colored supplement of the newspaper, he yawns, and he finally seeks relief from the mental vacuity of isolation by going where the combined mental vacuity of many partially relieves the mental vacuity of each particular individual.[49]

As evidenced by these quotations of Theodore Roosevelt it is quite clear that he was a devote Christian and a true biblical scholar. As president, he led the nation with true moral and ethical beliefs through some very troubling times. He should be counted as one of our great leaders and strong supporters of the Christian ethics that is missing today.

If ye know that he is righteous, ye know that every one that doeth righteousness is born of him.

−1 John 2:29 (KJV)

Woodrow Wilson 28th President of the United States (1856–1924)

Woodrow Wilson's father was a theologian and thus was raised in a very religious home. He remained deeply religious throughout his life. He was considered the most profoundly Christian political lead in the 20th century. He felt that he was following God's guidance. Wilson considered the United States to be a Christian nation destined to lead the world.

Quotations by Woodrow Wilson:

[The Bible is] a book which reveals men unto themselves, not as creatures in bondage, not as men under human authority, not as those bidden to take counsel and command of any human source. It reveals every man to himself as a distinct moral agent, responsible not to men, not even to those men whom he has put over him in authority, but responsible through his own conscience to his Lord and Maker. Whenever a man sees this vision he stands up a free man, whatever may be the government under which he lives, if he sees beyond the circumstances of his own life. –Speech on the tercentenary of the King James Bible, Denver, 7 May 1911

My life would not be worth living if it were not for the driving power of religion, for faith, pure and simple. I have seen all my life the arguments against it without ever having been moved by them...never for a moment have I had one doubt about my religious beliefs. There are people who believe only so far as they understand—that seems to me presumptuous and sets their understanding as the standard of the universe... I am sorry for such people. –Letter to Nancy Toy, 1915

It does not become America that within her borders, where every man is free to follow the dictates of his conscience, men should raise the cry of church against church. To do that is to strike at the very spirit and heart of America. –Speech, 4 November 1915

The Bible is the one supreme source of revelation of the meaning of life, the nature of God, and spiritual nature and needs of men. It is the only guide o life which really leads the spirit in the way of peace and salvation. America was born a Christian nation. America was born to exemplify that devotion to the elements of righteousness which are derived from the revelations of Holy Scripture.[50]

Woodrow Wilson who was also an historian and student of government stated:

The history of liberty is the history of resistance. The history of liberty is a history of the limitation of government power, not the increase of it. When we resist the concentration of power, we are resisting the powers of death. Concentration of power precedes the destruction of human liberties.

As you can see not only have we drifted away from Woodrow Wilson's vision of a spiritual America but also from his vision of a political America. Even though he was a Democrat politically he was also a Christian. He believed that a nation must lead the world through moral strength and the righteousness of our nation. This shows that the two ideologies do not have to be separate but can survive with the right spiritual leadership. With today's leadership it is not possible for the two to exist together. One must over power the other for this nation to either survive for the Glory of God or decline into oblivion.

I put on righteousness, and it clothed me: my judgment was as a robe and a diadem.

–Job 29:14 (KJV)

Calvin Coolidge 30th President of the United States (1872–1933)

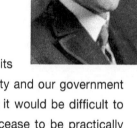

His full name was John Calvin Coolidge. A quiet and somber man whose sour expression masked a dry wit, Calvin Coolidge was known as "Silent Cal." After learning of his ascendancy to President on the death of Warren Harding in 1923, Coolidge was sworn in by his father, a justice of the peace, and promptly went back to bed.

Quotes by Calvin Coolidge:

The strength of our country is the strength of its religious conviction. The foundation of our society and our government rest so much on the teachings of the Bible that it would be difficult to support them if faith in these teachings would cease to be practically universal in our country

Our government rests upon religion. It is from that source that we derive our reverence for truth and justice, for equality and liberty, and for the rights of mankind. Unless the people believe in these principles they cannot believe in our government. There are only two main theories of government in the world. One rests on righteousness, the other rests on force. One appeals to reason, the other appeals to the sword. One is exemplified in a republic, the other is represented by a despotism.
–Speech at the unveiling of the equestrian statue of Bishop Francis Asbury, 15 October 1924

In this period of after war rigidity, suspicion, and intolerance our own country has not been exempt from unfortunate experiences. Thanks to our comparative isolation, we have known less of the international frictions and rivalries than some other countries less fortunately situated. But among some of the varying racial, religious, and social groups of our people there have been manifestations of an intolerance of opinion, a narrowness to outlook, a fixity of judgment, against which we may well be warned. It is not easy to conceive of anything that would be more unfortunate in a community based upon the ideals of which Americans boast than any considerable development of intolerance as regards religion. To a great extent this country owes its beginnings to the determination of our hardy ancestors to maintain complete freedom in religion. In stead of a state church we have decreed that every citizen shall be free to follow the dictates of his own conscience as to his religious beliefs and affiliations. Under that guaranty we have erected a system which certainly is justified by its fruits. Under no other could we have dared to invite the peoples of all countries and creeds to come here and unite with us in creating the State of which we are all citizens. –Speech before the American Legion Convention, 6 October 1925

Although I had been rather constant in my attendance, I had never joined the church... Among other things, I had some fear as to my ability to set that example which I always felt ought to denote the life of a church member. I am inclined to think now that this was the counsel of darkness. –Autobiography, 1929

Even though Calvin Coolidge was aware of the principles of Christianity and believed the nation should be led by Christian values, he himself was in the dark about what it takes to be a true Christian. Only through the Grace of God can we know for sure that the light of truth can dim the darkness of ignorance.

And the light shineth in darkness; and the darkness comprehended it not.
–John 1:5 (KJV)

Herbert C. Hoover 31st President of the United States (1874–1964)

Herbert Hoover was a Quaker and was raised in a religious family. He shared his views on religion and our nation in the following statements:

> For centuries, the human race believed that divine inspiration rested in a few. The result was blind faith in religious hierarchies, the Divine Right of Kings. The world has been disillusioned of this belief that divinity rests in any special group or class whether it be through a creed, a tyranny of kinds or of proletariat. Our individualism insists upon the divine in each human being. It rests upon the divine in each human being. It rests upon the firm faith that the divine spark can be awakened in every heart. It was the refusal to compromise these things that led to the migration of those religious groups who so largely composed our forefathers. Our diversified religious faiths are the apotheosis of spiritual individualism. --American Individualism, 1922

> I come of Quaker stock. My ancestors were persecuted for their beliefs. Here they sought and found religious freedom. By blood and conviction I stand for religious tolerance both in act and in spirit. –New Day, 1928

> The migration of our forefathers to America was in refuge from the continued regimentation of men and men's minds still frozen by classes, by feudalism, by the churches, and by governments. Liberty was already implicit in their religious beliefs and their spiritual aspirations. Their purpose was to establish it in government. –The Challenge to Liberty, 1934, p18

> This occasion is not alone the administration of the most sacred oath which can be assumed by an American citizen. *It is a dedication and consecration under God* to the highest office in service of our people. I assume this trust in the humility of knowledge that only through the guidance of Almighty Providence can I hope to discharge its ever-increasing burdens. I ask help of Almighty God in this service. –March 4, 1929 inaugural address. (emphasis added)

He also wrote:

The whole inspiration of our civilization springs from the teachings of Christ and the lessons of the prophets. To read the Bible for these fundamentals is a necessity of American life.

Then the deputy, when he saw what was done, believed, being astonished at the doctrine of the Lord.

–Acts 13:12 (KJV)

Franklin D. Roosevelt 32nd President of the United States (1882–1945)

Franklin Roosevelt was an Episcopalian and made the following statements regarding religion and our nation:

The lessons of religious toleration—a toleration which recognizes complete liberty of human thought, liberty of conscience —is one which, by precept and example, must be inculcated in the hearts and minds of all Americans if the institutions of our democracy are to be maintained and perpetuated.

We must recognize the fundamental rights of man. There can be no true national life in our democracy unless we give unqualified recognition to freedom of religious worship and freedom of education. –Letter to the Calvert Associates, 1937

The second is freedom of every person to worship God in his own way— everywhere in the world. –The "Four Freedoms" speech, 6 January 1941

He also stated:

We cannot read the history of our rise and development as a nation without reckoning with the place the Bible has occupied in shaping the advances of the Republic. Where we have been in the truest and most consistent in obeying its precepts, we have attained the greatest measure of contentment and prosperity.

These words are very true. As a nation, while still under the influence of the Bible and its teachings and laws, our nation prospered and grew like no other country in history. Once we begin turning away from the teachings of Christ our country begin to decline in world opinion and influence. Our nation is in a state of decline morally and economically. Is it just a coincidence that this has come at a time when Christianity is under attack?

The following excerpt from FDR's State of the Union address to Congress in 1939 underscores how, until recent years, America's leadership understood the vital connection between religion and democracy. With Hitler on the move in Europe, President Roosevelt said:

Storms from abroad directly challenge three institutions indispensable to Americans, now and always. The first is religion. It is the source of the other two—democracy and international good faith.

Religion, by teaching man his relationship to God, gives the individual a sense of his own dignity and teaches him to respect himself by respecting his neighbors.

...Where freedom of religion has been attacked, the attack has come from sources opposed to democracy. Where democracy has been overthrown, the spirit of free worship has disappeared. And where religion and democracy have vanished, good faith and reason in international affairs have given way to strident ambition and brute force.

An ordering of society which relegates religion, democracy, and good faith among nations to the background can find no place within it for the ideals of the Prince of Peace. The United States rejects such an ordering and retains it ancient faith..."[51]

As FDR said "...teaching man his relationship to God" is important to the survival of the soul of a nation. The soul of our nation is in dire jeopardy of being lost. We must all get back to the original intent of the Founding Fathers and live our lives for God and Country.

Harry S. Truman 33rd President of the United States (1884–1972)

Truman, a Southern Baptist, sought religious allies in the Cold War. He tried to unite the world's religions in a spiritual crusade against communism, sending his personal representative to Pope Pius XII to coordinate not only with the Vatican but also with the heads of the Anglican, Lutheran, and Greek Orthodox churches. "If I can mobilize the people who believe in a moral world against the Bolshevik materialists," Truman wrote in 1947, "we can win this fight"[52]

With the Cold War looming, President Truman saw the need to go to God for strength in dealing with evil. Just as his predecessors had sought wisdom from the teachings of Jesus Christ to keep our country on the path of righteousness through difficult times, Harry Truman too used his Baptist faith to strengthen his position on the world front.

In 1952 President Truman signed a bill establishing a National Day of Prayer to be called annually by the President of the United States.

> We have gone a long way toward civilization and religious tolerance, and we have a good example in this country. Here the many Protestant denominations, the Catholic Church and the Greek Orthodox Church do not seek to destroy one another in physical violence just because they do not interpret every verse of the Bible in exactly the same way. Here we now have the freedom of all religions, and I hope that never again will we have a repetition of religious bigotry, as we have had in certain periods of our own history. There is no room for that kind of foolishness here. –Mr. Citizen, 1960[53]
>
> The fundamental basis of this nation's laws was given to Moses on the Mount. The fundamental basis of our Bills of Rights comes from teachings we get from Exodus and Saint Matthew, from Isaiah and Saint Paul...If we don't have a proper fundamental moral background, we will finally end up with a totalitarian government which does not believe in rights for anybody except the State![54]

Harry Truman was right on the mark. Our nation is losing its moral background, and as a result we are facing the possibility of being taken over completely by a totalitarian government that is currently in power. We as a people have let our government usurp our rights in exchange for what the government chooses to dole out to us. Instead of relying on God and his mercy to provide for our nation the strength and moral character He demands, we have turned to the government to provide what it deems necessary.

We can see as a result of our country turning away from God we are in a very dangerous position in the world. We are being threatened by an evil force beyond most people comprehension. We are on the brink of war for our identity, for our beliefs, for religion, and for our very soul.

> *For the eyes of the LORD run to and fro throughout the whole earth, to shew himself strong in the behalf of them whose heart is perfect toward him. Herein thou hast done foolishly: therefore from henceforth thou shalt have wars.*
>
> **–2 Chronicles 16:9 (KJV)**

Dwight D. Eisenhower 34th President of the United States (1890–1969)

Eisenhower's family background was Mennonite (River Brethren) and became followers of the Watch Tower Society, whose members later took the name Jehovah's Witnesses. The Eisenhower home served as the local Watch Tower meeting Hall from 1896 to 1915, when Eisenhower's father stopped regularly associating due to the Watch Tower's failed prophesies that Armageddon would occur in October 1914 and 1915. Ike's father received a Watch Tower funeral when he died in the 1940s. Ike's mother continued as an active Jehovah's Witness until her death. Ike and his brothers also stopped associating regularly after 1915. In later years, Eisenhower was baptized, confirmed, and became a communicant in the Presbyterian church in a single ceremony on February 1, 1953, just weeks after his first inauguration as president. Eisenhower was the first president to officially join a church while in office.

In this way we are reaffirming the transcendence of religious faith in America's heritage and future; in this way we shall constantly strengthen those spiritual weapons which forever will be our country's most powerful resource in peace and war. –Flag Day speech, signing bill authorizing addition of the words "under God" to the Pledge of Allegiance, 14 June 1954.

We are particularly thankful to you for your part in the movement to have the words 'under God' added to our Pledge of Allegiance. These words will remind Americans that despite our great physical strength we must remain humble. They will help us to keep constantly in our minds and hearts the spiritual and moral principles which alone give dignity to man, and upon which our way of life is founded. For the contribution which your organization has made to this cause, we must be genuinely grateful. –Message to the Knights of Columbus meeting in Louisville, 17 August 1954[55]

Even as recently as 1954 our country was still living a good life based on the Judeo-Christian beliefs that our country was founded on. By adding the words "under God" to the Pledge of Allegiance reaffirmed that we still believed in what our Founding Fathers had pledged: "…And for the support of this Declaration, with a firm reliance on the protection of divine Providence, we mutually pledge to each other our Lives, our Fortunes and our sacred Honor."

Eisenhower also stated:

Without God there could be no American form of government, nor an American way of life. Recognition of the Supreme Being is the first, the most basic, expression of Americanism. Thus, the Founding Fathers of America saw it, and thus with God's help, it will continue to be.

Be ye mindful always of his covenant; the word which he commanded to a thousand generations;

–1 Chronicles 16:15 (KJV)

Ronald Reagan 40th President of the United States (1911–2004)

Ronald Reagan identified himself as a Presbyterian during most of his adult life. Reagan's father was a nominal Catholic. Reagan's mother was a devout member of the Disciples of Christ Church and Ronald Reagan was raised in the denomination. Reagan attended Eureka College, which is affiliated with the Disciples of Christ Church. Reagan himself became a Presbyterian as an adult. Reagan said that in temperament and religious beliefs he took after his mother.

For Reagan, spiritual faith was not something to hang in the closet upon taking political office. As governor he had often relied on prayer for guidance, and after entering the White House he felt he needed prayer as much as ever. And politics, he held, needed faith. He frequently invoked George Washington's aphorism that religion and morality were "indispensable supports" to political prosperity.

He also felt that America and Americans needed the Bible. The Bible, argued Reagan, held all the answers. "I'm accused of being simplistic at times," he said more than once. "But within that single Book are all the answers to all the problems that face us." As Ben Elliott remembers, it was a line that many found over-the-top, some White House staff among them. Nonetheless, Reagan believed it devoutly. When the president shared the thought before the National Religious Broadcasters convention, Elliott recalled, it "brought the house down." The audience responded with a standing ovation, and Reagan was delighted.

He saw God as the preeminent source of wisdom and moral guidance, the fount "from whom all knowledge springs." "When we open ourselves to Him," the president told a group of students in December 1983, "we gain not only moral courage but also intellectual strength." It was a line he had used for years.

In particular, Reagan believed that biblical wisdom was indispensable in devising intelligent law. One thing that "must never change" in America, he contended, is that men and women must "seek Divine guidance in the policies of their government and the promulgation of their laws." They must, he urged, "make our laws and government not only a model to mankind, but a testament to the wisdom and mercy of God."

A belief in the power of prayer, and an inclination to extend the lessons of religion to the challenges of policy: in these and other ways Ronald Reagan's spirituality shaped his presidency.[56]

...I am told that tens of thousands of prayer meetings are being held on this day, and for that I am deeply grateful. We are a nation under God, and I believe God intended for us to be free...our best effort, and our willingness to believe in ourselves and to believe in our capacity to perform great deeds; to believe that together, with God's help, we can and will resolve the problems which now confront us.

And, after all, why shouldn't we believe that? We are Americans. God bless you, and thank you. –President Ronald Reagan, 1981

In his second inaugural address Ronald Reagan said:

History is a ribbon, always unfurling; history is a journey. And as we continue our journey, we think of those who traveled before us. We stand together again at the steps of this symbol of our democracy—or we would have been standing at the steps if it hadn't gotten so cold. Now we are standing inside this symbol of our democracy. Now we hear again the echoes of our past: a general falls to his knees in the hard snow of Valley Forge; a lonely President paces the darkened halls, and ponders his struggle to preserve the Union; the men of the Alamo call out encouragement to each other; a settler pushes west and sings a song, and the song echoes out forever and fills the unknowing air.

It is the American sound. It is hopeful, big-hearted, idealistic, daring, decent, and fair. That's our heritage; that is our song. We sing it still. For all our problems, our differences, we are together as of old, as we raise our voices to the God who is the Author of this most tender music. And may He continue to hold us close as we fill the world with our sound—sound in unity, affection, and love—one people under God, dedicated to the dream of freedom that He has placed in the human heart, called upon now to pass that dream on to a waiting and hopeful world.

God bless you and may God bless America." –Ronald Reagan 1985

Other quotes by Ronald Reagan:

Freedom prospers when religion is vibrant and the rule of law under God is acknowledged.

Inside the Bible's pages lie all the to all the problems man has ever known...It is my firm belief that the enduring values presented in its pages have a great meaning for each of us and for our nation. The Bible can touch our hearts, order our minds, and refresh our souls.

Often called the "Book of Books", the Bible holds a unique place in American history, politics, religion, and popular culture. Unfortunately, though, biblical illiteracy is so prevalent today that when Reagan spoke so eloquently of a "shining city on a hill", few people realized he was referring to a sermon given by John Winthrop, the first governor of the Massachusetts Bay Colony, in 1630, which was based on the words of Jesus Christ in Matthew 5.

Ye are the light of the world. A city that is set on an hill cannot be hid.
–Matthew 5:14 (KJV)

In this "shining city on a hill" speech given in 1974 Reagan concluded by saying:

We cannot escape our destiny, nor should we try to do so. The leadership of the free world was thrust upon us two centuries ago in that little hall of Philadelphia. In the days following World War II, when the economic strength and power of America was all that stood between the world and the return to the dark ages, Pope Pius XII said, "The American people have a great genius for splendid and unselfish actions. Into the hands of America God has placed the destinies of an afflicted mankind."
We are indeed, and we are today, the last best hope for man on earth.

For whatsoever things were written aforetime were written for our learning, that we through patience and comfort of the scriptures might have hope.
–Romans 15:4 (KJV)

As Reagan said, "If we ever forget that we are One Nation Under God, then we will be a nation gone under." Only through the Word of God can we remain true to Him. Those who ignore His Word are doomed to a life unfulfilled.

So are the paths of all that forget God; and the hypocrite's hope shall perish:

–Job 8:13 (KJV)

George H. W. Bush 41st President of the United States (1924–)

George Herbert Walker Bush was born June 12, 1924, in Milton, Mass., to Prescott and Dorothy Bush. The family later moved to Connecticut. The youth studied at the elite Phillips Academy in Andover, Mass.

George Bush was a former World War II pilot, Texas oil tycoon, Republican congressman, U.N. ambassador and Director of the Central Intelligence Agency before serving as vice president under Ronald Reagan.

The future president joined the Navy after war broke out and at 18 became the Navy's youngest commissioned pilot, serving from 1942 to 1945, and was awarded the Distinguished Flying Cross. He fought the Japanese on 58 missions and was shot down once.

George H. W. Bush brought to the White House a dedication to traditional American values and a determination to direct them toward making the United States "a kinder and gentler nation." In his Inaugural Address he pledged in "a moment rich with promise" to use American strength as "a force for good."

George H. W. Bush was an Episcopalian. He attended St. John's Episcopal Church while he was President.

In his 1989 Inaugural Address he stated:

...And my first act as President is a prayer, I ask you to bow your heads:

Heavenly Father, we bow our heads and thank You for Your love. Accept our thanks for the peace that yields this day and the shared faith that makes its continuance likely. Make us strong to do Your work, willing to heed and hear Your will, and write on our hearts these words: "Use power to help people." For we are given power not to advance our own purpose, nor to make a great show in the world, nor a name. There is but one just use of power, and it is to serve people. Help us remember it, Lord. Amen

But so shall it not be among you: but whosoever will be great among you, shall be your minister:44 And whosoever of you will be the chiefest, shall be servant of all. 45 For even the Son of man came not to be ministered unto, but to minister, and to give his life a ransom for many.

–Mark 10:43-45 (KJV)

When George Bush was campaigning for the presidency, as incumbent vice-president, one of his stops was in Chicago, Illinois, on August 27, 1987. At O'Hare Airport he held a formal outdoor news conference. There Robert I. Sherman, a reporter for the American Atheist news journal, fully accredited by the state of Illinois and by invitation a participating member of the press corps covering the national candidates, had the following exchange with then Vice-President Bush.

Sherman: What will you do to win the votes of the Americans who are atheists?

Bush: I guess I'm pretty weak in the atheist community. Faith in God is important to me.

Sherman: Surely you recognize the equal citizenship and patriotism of Americans who are atheists?

Bush: No, I don't know that atheists should be considered as citizens, nor should they be considered patriots. This is one nation under God.

Sherman (somewhat taken aback): Do you support as a sound constitutional principle the separation of state and church?

Bush: Yes, I support the separation of church and state. I'm just not very high on atheists.[57]

Quotes by George H. W. Bush:

I am guided by certain traditions. One is that there is a God and He is good, and his love, while free, has a self imposed cost: We must be good to one another. –Convention Acceptance, 1988

As I said many times before, prayer always has been important in our lives. And without it, I really am convinced, more and more convinced, that no man or no woman who has the privilege of serving in the

Presidency could carry out their duties without prayer. –Remarks to the National Association of Evangelicals in Chicago, Illinois, 3 March 1992

I am very disappointed by the Supreme Court's decision in Lee v. Weisman. The Court said that a simple nondenominational prayer thanking God for the liberty of America at a public school graduation ceremony violates the first amendment. America is a land of religious pluralism, and this is one of our Nation's greatest strengths. While we must remain neutral toward particular religions and protect freedom of conscience, we should not remain neutral toward religion itself. In this case, I believe that the Court has unnecessarily cast away the venerable and proper American tradition of nonsectarian prayer at public celebrations. I continue to believe that this type of prayer should be allowed in public schools. –Statement on the Supreme Court Decision on the Lee v. Weisman Case, 24 June 1992

Americans are the most religious people on Earth. And we have always instinctively sensed that God's purpose was bound up with the cause of liberty. The Founders understood this. As Jefferson put it, "Can the liberties of a nation be thought secure when we have removed their only firm basis, a conviction in the minds of the people that these liberties are the gift of God?" That conviction is enshrined in our Declaration of Independence and in our Constitution. And it's no accident that in drafting our Bill of Rights, the Founders dedicated the first portion of our first amendment to religious liberty. We rightly emphasize the opening clause of that amendment, which forbids government from establishing religion. In fact, I believe the establishment clause has been a great boon to our country's religious life. One reason religion flourishes in America is that worship can never be controlled by the state.

But in recent times we have too often ignored the clause that follows, which forbids government from prohibiting the free exercise of religion. This myopia has in some places resulted in an aggressive campaign against religious belief itself. Some people seem to believe that freedom of religion requires government to keep our lives free from religion. Well, I believe they're just plain wrong. Our government was founded on faith. Government must never promote a religion, of course, but it is duty bound to promote religious liberty. And it must never put the believer at a disadvantage because of his belief. That is the challenge that our administration has undertaken. To be succinct, it is my conviction that children have a right to voluntary prayer in the public schools. –Remarks to the National Association of Evangelicals in Chicago, Illinois,

George H. W. Bush also stated:

The great faith that led our nation's Founding Fathers to pursue this bold experience in self-government has sustained us in uncertain and perilous times; it has given us strength and inspiration to this very day.

President Bush, even though a very wealthy man, never let his wealth interfere with is love of God or his country. He always made decisions based on his moral and religious values learned in his youth. He believed that this nation was founded in the principles of the teachings of Jesus Christ. He believed America is "One Nation Under God".

Charge them that are rich in this world, that they be not highminded, nor trust in uncertain riches, but in the living God, who giveth us richly all things to enjoy;

–1 Timothy 6:17 (KJV)

George W. Bush 43rd President of the United States (1946–)

George W. Bush is a Methodist by religion and he is the third well-known Methodist who has held the highest office in the nation. The others were Rutherford B. Hayes and William McKinley.

George W. Bush and Rutherford B. Hayes are also linked by a historical oddity; each lost the popular vote, yet won the presidency after a contested dispute over balloting in Florida.

You might think the election of another Methodist would be a source of pride for the United Methodist Church. In a remarkable display of candor, the United Methodist News Service instead detailed the president-elect's political differences with the denomination. It even pointed out that Mr. Bush's political views have often been compared to those of a rival denomination, the Southern Baptist Convention.

Though he was raised in Presbyterian and Episcopalian churches, Mr. Bush has been an active Methodist since quitting alcohol and finding God in 1985. He and his wife Laura have taught Sunday school at Highland Park United Methodist Church in Dallas, and while he was governor of Texas he worshiped at the Tarrytown United Methodist Church in Austin.

Mr. Bush has frequently spoken about religion in terms rarely associated with members of mainline Protestant denominations in New England. He says he was born again after talking to Billy Graham, he has named Jesus as his favorite political philosopher, and has questioned whether non-Christians can go to heaven. Church officials say such talk would be quite familiar to Methodists in Texas and other parts of the south.[58]

In the spring of 1999, as George W. Bush prepared to announce his run for president, he agreed to be interviewed about his religious faith. However, he said, "I want people to judge me on my deeds, not how I try to define myself as a religious person of words," he said. Since taking office however, Bush's personal faith turned highly public, arguably more so than any modern president. It's not just that Bush is talking about God, but that he's talking about God differently. Bush has made several statements indicating he believes God is involved in world events and that he and America have a divinely guided mission.

After Bush's Sept. 20, 2001, speech to Congress, Bush speechwriter Mike Gerson called the president and said: "Mr. President, when I saw you on television, I thought, 'God wanted you there.'" "He wants us all here, Gerson," the president responded. In that speech Bush said, "Freedom and fear, justice and cruelty, have always been at war, and we know that God is not neutral between them." The implication: God will intervene on the world stage, mediating between good and evil.

At a National Prayer Breakfast, for instance, Bush said: "We can be confident in the ways of Providence… Behind all of life and all of history, there's a dedication and purpose, set by the hand of a just and faithful God."

At the prayer breakfast, during which he talked about God's impact on history, Bush also said he felt "the presence of the Almighty" while comforting the families of the astronauts of Space Shuttle Columbia during the Houston memorial service Feb. 4, 2003.

In his State of the Union address in 2003, Bush said the nation puts its confidence in the loving God "behind all of life and all of history" and that "we go forward with confidence, because this call of history has come to the right country. May He guide us now."

In addition to these public statements indicating a divine intervention in world events, there is evidence Bush believes his election as president was a result of God's acts. A month after the World Trade Center attack, World magazine, a conservative Christian publication, quoted Tim Goeglein, deputy director of White House public liaison, saying: "I think President Bush is God's man at this hour, and I say this with a great sense of humility." Time magazine reported, "Privately, Bush even talked of being chosen by the grace of God to lead at that moment."

It's even possible that Bush's belief in America's moral rightness makes the country's military threats seem more genuine because the world thinks Bush is "on a mission."

Presidents always have used Scripture in their speeches as a source of poetry and morality, according to Michael Waldman, President Clinton's chief speechwriter, author of "POTUS Speaks", and now a visiting professor at Harvard's Kennedy School of Government. Lincoln, he said, was the first president to use the Bible extensively in his speeches. One of the main reasons was that his audience knew the Bible; Lincoln was using what was then common language. Theodore Roosevelt, in his 1912 speech to the Progressive Party, closed with these words: "We stand at the edge of Armageddon." Presidents Carter, Reagan and Clinton all used Scripture.

Bush is different, Waldman said, because he uses theology as the guts of his argument. "That's very unusual in the long sweep of American history."

George W. Bush, known in some circles as a Presidential Preacher, is among the most openly religious presidents in U.S. history. A daily Bible reader, he often talks about how Jesus changed his heart. He has spoken, publicly and privately, of hearing God's call to run for the presidency and of praying for God's help while he was in office. He has said many times that he is a Christian, believes in the power of prayer and considers himself a "lowly sinner."[59]

Quotes by George W. Bush:

Our Founding Fathers recognized that religious freedom is a right we must protect with great vigilance. We must continue our efforts to uphold justice and tolerance and to oppose prejudice; and we must be resolved to countering any means that infringe on religious freedom.

Prayer is an opportunity to praise God for His mighty works, His gift of freedom, His mercy, and His boundless love. Through prayer, we recognize the limits of earthly power and acknowledge the sovereignty of God. According to Scripture, 'the Lord is near to all who call upon Him...He also will hear their cry, and save them.' Prayer leads to humility and a grateful heart, and it turns our minds to the needs of others.

On September 11, 2001, in addressing the American people, President Bush stated:

...America was targeted for attack because we're the brightest beacon for freedom and opportunity in the world. These attacks shattered steel, but they cannot dent the steel of American resolve... Today, our nation saw evil, the very worst of human nature. And we respond with the best of America...This is the day all Americans from every walk of life unite in our resolve for justice and peace...we go forward to defend freedom and all that is good and just in our world.

President George W. Bush truly believes that God will protect our country as long as we believe the truth of the Bible and the teaching of Jesus Christ. He believes we are fighting a battle, not just our country and way of life, but for the very soul of our nation. We are in a battle between good and evil.

Put on the whole armour of God, that ye may be able to stand against the wiles of the devil. 12 For we wrestle not against flesh and blood, but against principalities, against powers, against the rulers of the darkness of this world, against spiritual wickedness in high places.
–Ephesians 6:11-12 (KJV)

How can we doubt that our nation was founded on Judeo-Christian beliefs? The words of our Founding Fathers, in their writings, both public and private, show the truth of their beliefs. They were Christians! Most of our national leaders that have followed them, no matter what political party, conservative or liberal, also show they too are Christians and believe that this nation should not turn away from God and His Teachings and His Laws. In times of strife and sorrow, in peace or in war, our leaders have shown how the word of our Lord has strengthened them and how God has helped to protect our nation.

We must, as a nation, put the Lord Jesus Christ and his teachings, and the Laws of God back in the foundation of our government; local, state, and national. We must not turn our back on God or he surely will turn is back on us. We must, as a nation, ask God for His forgiveness and blessings and go forward in his name, else we risk loosing his Grace and be judged as the sinners we are and be left on our own path only to be lost and alone.

But let him ask in faith, nothing wavering. For he that wavereth is like a wave of the sea driven with the wind and tossed.

–James 1:6 (KJV)

Article One, Section 7 of the United States Constitution states:

...If any Bill shall not be returned by the President within ten Days **(Sundays excepted)** after it shall have been presented to him..." (emphasis added)

This clearly shows that the Founding Fathers were concerned for Christianity's recognition of Sunday being the Sabbath day and a day of rest, according to God's Law. Every president has concurred with this section of the Constitution until recently when President Barack Obama sign the health care bill into law on a ***Sunday night***, ignoring history, the Constitution, and the Bible.

Chapter Three

EDUCATING A
CHRISTIAN NATION

E ducation was considered mainly a family or local responsibility, not an obligation of the state. In the Land Ordinance of 1785, Congress decreed that a section of every township surveyed in the public lands in the western territories be set aside for the maintenance of public schools. The Northwest Ordinance of 1787 provided land for education in the Great Lakes and Ohio Valley regions. However, neither ordinance was fully implemented. Some leaders were already calling out for educating the citizenry of the new nation.

Thomas Jefferson proclaimed that **"If a nation expects to be ignorant and free, it expects what never was and never will be."** Benjamin Rush and Noah Webster were two more voices of the time advocating an educated populace for the republic. It would be quite awhile before their ideas would be put into action. Schooling was conducted in the home or in small one-room school houses. The curriculum centered on the "3r's" along with moral and religious training. **The purpose of learning to read was to be able to read the Bible for oneself.**

Sometimes citizens of a local community would band together to hire a teacher to instruct their children. The teacher, usually a man, would be paid little, often have only a rudimentary education himself, and be boarded at a home in the community. Washington Irving's Ichabod Crane, of headless horseman fame, is an example of such a school teacher. On the isolated farms of the frontier, no formal education was available and the children were taught by their parents, if at all. Teaching the skills of farming for the boys and homemaking for the girls was considered the main priority. Wealthy families hired tutors for their young children and sent the older ones to private schools and then on to college. Massachusetts led the way in public financing for education. In 1800 its legislature gave local school districts the power to levy taxes. In 1805 the New York Free School Society was founded by Mayor DeWitt Clinton, for the purpose of establishing "Free School for the Education of Poor children who do not belong to, or are not provided for, by any Religious Society." The society had the novel idea of training its teachers and instituted a six to eight week training program for them.[60]

Most of America's oldest universities were started by preachers and churches. Harvard, Yale, William and Mary, Princeton, King's College (now Columbia University), Brown, Rutgers, and Dartmouth were all founded by Christian preachers and church affiliations.

Harvard University, for example, was founded in 1636 by the Puritans, adopted the "Rules and Precepts" of the university that stated: **"Let every student be plainly instructed, and earnestly pressed to consider well, the main end of his life and studies is, to know God and Jesus Christ which is eternal life and therefore lay Christ at the bottom, as the only foundation of all sound knowledge and learning."** Even Harvard's original seal, which can be seen etched in the walls of the campus today, states upon it these words: **"Truth for Christ and the Church."**

Yale College was established in 1701 with a stated goal that **"every student shall consider the main end of his study to wit to know God in Jesus Christ and answerably to lead a godly, sober life."** The College of William and Mary was founded in 1693 to supply the church of Virginia **"with a seminary of ministers"** that the **"Christian faith may be propagated."** And King's College, known today as Columbia University, purposed to **"inculcate upon students' tender minds the great principles of Christianity and morality."** Princeton had as one of its founding statements: **"Cursed is all learning that is contrary to the Cross of Christ."**

Look at these universities today and see how far they have fallen from their original charters, to be sure, some the graduates have fallen from God.

In Colonial America, in addition to the Bible and the "Bay Psalm Book," the first textbook for schoolchildren, "The New England Primer", taught the ABC's by children memorizing basic biblical truths and lessons about life: A– "In Adam's fall, we sinned all." B– "Heaven to find, the Bible Mind." C– Christ crucify'd for sinners died," and so on. Included in the "Primer" were the names of the Old and New Testament books, the Lord's Prayer, the Apostles' Creed, the Ten Commandments, and other religious references. The "Primer" was the second best-selling book in the American colonies, the Bible was number one.[61]

First introduced in Boston in 1690, "The New England Primer" was a school book from which Americans learned to read until 1930; it is what would today be described as a first grade textbook. Not only were many of the Founding Fathers raised on this textbook but they even reprinted it to make sure it was available for children in their generation.

Considering the educational system and textbooks that produced our Founding Fathers, no wonder so many were Christians and were outspoken about the importance of Christian principles in American government.

During the powerful evangelical revivals of the "Second Great Awakening" many benevolent societies were formed. They included "The American Education Society" (1815), "The American Bible Society" (1816), "The American Sunday School Society" (1824), "The American Tract Society" (1825), and "The American Missionary Society" (1826). These societies had local branches existing in almost every town and city. All of them were voluntary, devoutly Christian, and many had no ties to any single religious group. Most were interdenominational, and cooperative enterprises often took place among the societies.

The "Mississippi Valley Plan," devised by John Beck to evangelize the upper Mississippi Valley in 1826, shows how these agencies worked together. He went to the Baptist General Convention and the American Home Missionary Society and convinced them that every missionary could sell Bibles for the American Bible Society, distribute tracts for the American Tract Society, and start Sunday schools for the American Sunday School Union. The agencies adopted the plan, and as a result, 23,000 Bibles and $18,000 worth of tracts were shipped to Ohio and Kentucky in 1830 alone.

The "Mississippi Valley Enterprise" (MVE), which was a missionary enterprise of the "American Sunday School Union", was formed to establish a Sunday school in every impoverished area throughout the entire Mississippi Valley. The MVE established over sixty one thousand Sunday schools and enrolled 2,650,000 pupils in fifty years. One missionary named Stephen Paxton started 1,314 Sunday schools with 83,000 students during his twenty years of service to the mission.

Members of these societies considered themselves as American patriots who believed in the views of the Founding Fathers, that religion was a necessary source for republican government. These societies assumed the role of helping to form the virtuous citizenry of which the Founding Fathers spoke. The conversion of souls was also seen as helping to save the republic. For instance, the American Home Missionary Society assured its supporters in 1826, that they were doing the work of patriotism no less than Christianity.

> *I have shewed you all things, how that so labouring ye ought to support the weak, and to remember the words of the Lord Jesus, how he said, It is more blessed to give than to receive.*
>
> **–Acts 20:35 (KJV)**

Thomas Jefferson—3rd President of the United States (1743–1826)

Thomas Jefferson was a strong advocate of education. He felt that and education citizenry was protection against tyranny. He stated:

> If a nation expects to be ignorant and free, in a state of civilization, it expects what never was and never will be.
>
> ...whenever the people are well-informed, they can be trusted with their own government; that, whenever things get so far wrong as to attract their notice, they may be relied on to set them right.

The above quotes were the cornerstones of Jefferson's interest in education. He placed education as the foundation of democracy and a prerequisite to vote.

Ignorance and sound self-government could not exist together: the one destroyed the other. A despotic government could restrain its citizens and deprive the people of their liberties only while they were ignorant.

Jefferson could never completely separate education from government. With the fullest faith in the ability of man to govern himself, Jefferson nonetheless realized the responsibility of self-government could be assumed successfully only by an enlightened people.[62]

Francis Asbury (1745–1816)

Francis Asbury was a Methodist circuit rider (preacher on horseback) who traveled nearly three hundred thousand miles on horseback and preached more than sixteen thousand sermons from 1771 to 1816. Led by Asbury, an army of circuit riders were inspired to go where the pioneers went. In this forty-five year period, the Methodists grew in number from only three hundred members with four ministers to over 200,000 with 2,000 ministers, many with little formal education but who spoke the language of the frontier people.

Just as John the Baptist was proclaiming the coming of Christ and the repentance of sin, these circuit riders were going around the country preaching the Word of God and telling people to repent their sins and believe on the Lord Jesus Christ.

In those days came John the Baptist, preaching in the wilderness of Judaea, And saying, Repent ye: for the kingdom of heaven is at hand.
—Matthew 3:1-2 (KJV)

At the same time, the Baptists sent out their "farmer-preachers". As with the Methodists, the Baptists developed systems that made it easy for committed laypeople to enter the ministry and to be deployed quickly where the greatest opportunities were. With an emphasis on the need for a personal conversion and salvation from sin through faith in Jesus Christ, these ministers spread the Gospel far and wide.

As was true in the founding of the American colonies, Christians planted many of America's colleges as the nation moved west, including Northwestern University in Chicago, which was founded by the Methodists, and the University of California at Berkeley, which was founded by the Presbyterians before becoming a state university.[63]

Notice how things have changed with these universities. Most notably, UC at Berkeley, which has become a hotbed of liberalism and godlessness.

Fisher Ames (1758–1808)

Fisher Ames was a Founder and politician who helped formulate the Bill of Rights, stated:

> We have a dangerous trend beginning to take place in our education. We're starting to put more and more textbooks into our schools...We've become accustomed of late of putting little books into the hands of our children containing fable and moral lessons...
>
> We are spending less time in the classroom on the Bible, which should be the principal text of our schools...The Bible states these great moral lessons better than any other manmade book.[64]

Wherewithal shall a young man cleanse his way? by taking heed thereto according to thy word.

–Psalms 119:9 (KJV)

Noah Webster (The Father of American Education)

Noah Webster expressed the purpose of schools was meant for the advancement of the Christian faith. He said in the Preface to the Noah Webster Dictionary, 1828:

> In my view, the Christian religion is the most important and one of the first things in which all children, under a free government ought to be instructed...No truth is more evident to my mind than that the Christian religion must be the basis of any government intended to secure the rights and privileges of a free people.

Webster also said:

> Education is useless without the Bible. The Bible was American's basic text book in all fields. God's Word, contained in the Bible, has furnished all necessary rules to direct our conduct.

Webster believed that a well educated society was essential to the preservation of freedom. He wrote: *"Information is fatal to despotism"*. Part of his life was spent writing and publishing textbooks to be used in local schools and homes, that would convey the basics of spelling and grammar, as well as provide both moral and civic education.

He wrote:

An attempt to conduct the affairs of a free government with wisdom and impartiality, and to preserve the just rights of all classes of citizens, without guidance of Divine precepts, will certainly end in disappointment. God is the supreme moral Governor of the world He has made, and as He Himself governs with perfect rectitude, He requires His rational creatures to govern themselves in like manner. If men will not submit to be controlled by His laws, He will punish them by the evils resulting from their own disobedience...

In my view, the Christian religion is the most important and one of the first things in which all children, under a free government ought to be instructed...No truth is more evident to my mind than that the Christian religion must be the basis of any government intended to secure the rights and privileges of a free people.

As one of America's founders, he knew that an education devoid of religious training was defective.

Webster was right on target. As anyone can see in today's society, now that God has left the classroom, we are experiencing one of the most difficult times in our nation's history. We have high unemployment and people losing their homes at a record rate. The educational standards in our schools have been lowered to make it easier for those too lazy, or who don't care, to pass from one grade to another. The high school graduation rates in our country have plummeted to historic lows. There is no moral leadership in our schools leaving the students to fend for themselves in the matters of morality and ethics.

With one generation after another being deprived of God's Word in the class room, is it any wonder that the young parents of today don't really know how to teach morals or ethics to their children? Without the moral guidance of the teachers the students are left to only wonder. Without God's direction the students are lost.

And all thy children shall be taught of the LORD; and great shall be the peace of thy children.

–Isaiah 54:13 (KJV)

Till I come, give attendance to reading, to exhortation, to doctrine.

–1 Timothy 4:13 (KJV)

William Samuel Johnson (1727–1819)

William Samuel Johnson was the son of Samuel Johnson, the first president of King's College (later Columbia College and University). William was born at Stratford, CT, in 1727. His father, who was a well-known Anglican clergyman-philosopher, prepared him for college and he graduated from Yale in 1744. About 3 years later he received a master of arts degree from the same institution and an honorary master's from Harvard.

Resisting his father's wish that he become a minister, Johnson embraced law instead—largely by educating himself and without benefit of formal training.

Johnson did not shirk the civic responsibilities of one of his station. In the 1750s he began his public career as a Connecticut militia officer. In 1761 and 1765 he served in the lower house of the Colonial assembly. In 1766 and 1771 he was elected to the upper house. At the time of the Revolution, Johnson was disturbed by conflicting loyalties. Although he attended the Stamp Act Congress in 1765, moderately opposed the Townshend Duties of 1767, and believed that most British policies were unwise, he retained strong transatlantic ties and found it difficult to choose sides. Many of his friends resided in Britain; in 1765 and 1766 Oxford University conferred honorary master's and doctor's degrees upon him; he had a strong association with the Anglican Church.

Johnson finally decided to work for peace between Britain and the colonies and to oppose the extremist Whig faction. On that basis, he refused to participate in the First Continental Congress, to which he was elected in 1774, following service as a judge of the Connecticut Colonial supreme court (1772-74). When hostilities broke out, he confined his activities to peacemaking efforts. In April 1775 Connecticut sent him and another emissary to speak to British Gen. Thomas

Gage about ending the bloodshed. But the time was not ripe for negotiations and they failed. Johnson fell out of favor with radical patriot elements who gained the ascendancy in Connecticut government and they no longer called upon his service. Although he was arrested in 1779 on charges of communicating with the enemy, he cleared himself and was released.

Once the passions of war had ebbed, Johnson resumed his political career. In the Continental Congress (1785-87), he was one of the most influential and popular delegates. Playing a major role in the Constitutional Convention, he missed no sessions after arriving on June 2, espoused the Connecticut Compromise, and chaired the Committee of Style which shaped the final document. He also worked for ratification in Connecticut.

Johnson took part in the new government, in the U.S. Senate where he contributed to passage of the Judiciary Act of 1789. In 1791, the year after the government moved from New York to Philadelphia, he resigned mainly because he preferred to devote all his energies to the presidency of Columbia College (1787-1800), in New York City. During these years, he established the school on a firm basis and recruited a fine faculty.[65]

William Samuel Johnson, as president of Columbia University, said to the first graduating class after the Revolutionary War:

You have received a public education, the purpose whereof hath been to qualify you the better to serve your Creator and your country... Your first great duties are those you owe to Heaven, to your Creator and Redeemer.

The words of William Johnson **should** be the same today as they were 280 years ago! However, because omitting God from our schools and other public areas, we have reached a place that will be hard to return from if we do not bring our Lord, our Creator, and our Redeemer back into the classroom. For without God in our lives and our classrooms our path can only lead to sin and sorrow. We must teach our children to seek Salvation from our Lord or we can only see them in the ranks of the wicked.

Salvation is far from the wicked: for they seek not thy statutes.
–Psalms 119:155 (KJV)

Dr. Benjamin Rush (1746–1813)

Dr. Benjamin Rush was one of the most influential Founding Fathers. He was one the first Founders to call for free, national, public schools. A distinguished physician and scientist, he knew of the importance of educating the citizens of the nation regarding the stability of the country. He stated:

I believe no man was ever early instructed in the truths of the Bible without having been made wiser or better by the early operation of these impressions of the mind...

If moral precepts alone could have reformed mankind, the mission of the Son of God into our world would have been unnecessary. He came to promulgate a system of doctrines, as well as a system of morals...it fixes upon the eternal and self-moving principle of LOVE. It concentrates a whole system of ethics in a single text of Scripture: **"A new commandment I give unto you, that ye love one another, even as I have loved you."** By withholding the knowledge of this doctrine from children, we deprive ourselves of the best means of awakening moral sensibility in their minds...(emphasis added)

Beloved, let us love one another: for love is of God; and every one that loveth is born of God, and knoweth God.

–1 John 4:7 (KJV)

William Holms McGuffey (1800–1873)

William Holms McGuffey was considered the "Schoolmaster of the Nation", published the first edition of the "McGuffey Reader" in 1836, one of the nation's first and most widely used series of textbooks in public education. It is estimated that at least 120 million copies of "McGuffey Readers" were sold between 1836 and 1960, placing its sales in a category with the Bible and "Webster's Dictionary".

McGuffey wrote:

Selections have been made drawn from the purest fountains of English literature...Copious extracts made from the Sacred Scripture.

Upon a review of the work...an apology may be due for not having still more liberally transferred to pages the chaste simplicity, the thrilling pathos, the living descriptions, and the matchless sublimity of the Sacred Writings.

From no source has the author drawn more copiously than from the Sacred Scriptures...In a Christian country, that a man is to be pitied, who, at this day, can honestly object to imbuing the minds of youth with the language and spirit of the Word of God." 1

For whatsoever things were written aforetime were written for our learning, that we through patience and comfort of the scriptures might have hope.

–Romans 15:4 (KJV)

Woodrow Wilson 28th President of the United States (1856–1924)

Woodrow Wilson stated:

Every Sunday school should be a place where this great book (the Bible) is not only opened, is not only studied, is not only revered, but is drunk of as if it were a fountain of life...No great nation can ever survive its own temptations and its own follies that does not indoctrinate its children in the Word of God; so that as schoolmaster and as Governor I know that my feet must rest with the feet of my fellowmen upon this foundation...for the righteousness of nations, like the righteousness of men, must take its source from these foundations of inspiration.

Preach the word; be instant in season, out of season; reprove, rebuke, exhort with all longsuffering and doctrine.

–2 Timothy 4:2 (KJV)

Chapter Four

THE DECLINE OF
A CHRISTIAN NATION

My father, Howard Stevens, was in the Army during World War II. He served in both the European Theater of war and also the South Pacific Theater of war. Each time he shipped out for one of those destinations he and all of the other soldiers were given a small 8" X 14" American flag so they could keep it with them while fighting our enemies. (I currently have one of his flags framed and mounted on my office wall.) The soldiers were also given a small pocket sized Bible to help them in their spiritual fight. This is when America was fighting for its very survival and the survival of the free world. This is when America was still considered a Christian nation.

In 1954, under the direction of President Dwight D. Eisenhower, our nation reaffirmed our belief in the principles of our Founding Fathers. We were founded in the establishment of Judeo-Christian value. Two simple words were added to our Pledge of Allegiance; *"Under God"*. This truly shows that the people of this great nation were still on the moral footing established by God.

This was a time of plenty and happiness in America. We maintained the moral compass established by the teachings of Jesus Christ. As we prospered as a nation, we also grew closer to God. God was everywhere; our homes, our courthouses, and our buildings of government. Our churches were sacrosanct, our homes were blessed, and our leadership was all about the people… Or so we thought!

> *But if it be of God, ye cannot overthrow it; lest haply ye be found even to fight against God.*
>
> **–Acts 5:39 (KJV)**

We were going on our daily lives, living in a free society that allowed the freedom to practice our religion as we saw fit. A society not influenced by a government that was against any form of religious expression. A society that was not bombarded with news and advertising full of sex and violence. Yes, we were at peace with ourselves, and at peace with the Lord… Or so we thought!

It was during this time that challenges to our religious freedom were beginning to be made in our courts. Most people of that time did not realize what was going on and the newspapers did not always write headline stories concerning these legal challenges. The average religious person of this country was not aware of these issues. This was the beginning of taking God out of the public domain and trying to force Him into the back alleys of society. This is when the courts had started to overturn all precedents set by earlier court decisions to uphold Christianity as a way of life.

> *And said to the judges, Take heed what ye do: for ye judge not for man, but for the LORD, who is with you in the judgment.*
>
> **–2 Chronicles 19:6 (KJV)**

THE CASE AGAINST A CHRISTIAN NATION

Cantwell vs Connecticut, 310 U.S. 296 (1940)

This was a case heard by the U. S. Supreme Court in 1940. Three Jehovah's Witnesses were arrested and charged with disorderly conduct and unlawful solicitation after trying to proclaim their faith on public sidewalks. The solicitation ordinance under which the Witnesses were charged was struck down by the Supreme Court, stating: **"To condition the solicitation of aid for the perpetuation of religious views is to lay a forbidden burden upon the exercise of liberty protected by the Constitution."** This case is significant because it is the first case to hold that the religious clauses of the First Amendment are fundamental rights guaranteed by the United States Constitution.

While we were going along our peaceful way, Satan was hard a work using the highest court in the land to do his bidding. The Supreme Court of the United States of America.

In order to understand the nature of the cases brought before the U. S. Supreme Court concerning religion one must first understand the origin and meaning of the Establishment Clause and the Free Exercise Clause stated in the First Amendment to the U. S. Constitution.

Two clauses of the First Amendment concern the relationship of government to religion: the Establishment Clause and the Free Exercise Clause. The First Amendment to the U.S. Constitution begins with the phrase "Congress shall make no law respecting an establishment of religion…" This phrase is referred to as the establishment clause. The Free Exercise Clause is the remainder of that phrase, "… or prohibiting the free exercise thereof." Although the clauses were intended by the framers to serve common values, there is some tension between the two. For example, some people might suggest that providing a military chaplain for troops stationed overseas violates the Establishment Clause, while others might suggest that *failing to provide* a chaplain violates the Free Exercise Clause rights of the same troops.

At an absolute minimum, the Establishment Clause was intended to prohibit the federal government from declaring and financially supporting a national religion, such as existed in many other countries at the time of the nation's founding. It is far less clear whether the Establishment Clause was also intended to prevent the federal government from supporting Christianity in general. Proponents of a narrow interpretation of the clause point out that the same First Congress that proposed the Bill of Rights also opened its legislative day with prayer and voted to apportion federal dollars to establish Christian missions in the Indian lands. On the other hand, persons seeing a far broader meaning in the clause point to writings by Thomas Jefferson and James Madison suggesting the need to establish "a wall of separation" between church and state.[68]

Neither Thomas Jefferson nor James Madison suggested that the separation between church and state meant that the country was to be free **from** religion. They wanted to make sure the government would not control religion, nor **prohibit** religion.

Supreme Court interpretation of the Establishment Clause does not begin until 1947 in *Everson v Board of Education*. Voting 5 to 4, the Court upheld a state law that *reimbursed parents* for the cost of busing their children to parochial schools. (It was clear from the various opinions in *Everson* that if the state had reimbursed the parochial schools for the cost of providing the transportation, that it would have been found to violate the Establishment Clause.) Although in his majority opinion Justice Black wrote of the "wall of separation" that the Constitution maintains between church and state, Black viewed the aid in question of serving the state's secular interest in getting kids "safely and expeditiously" to schools. The case is noteworthy for its extensive discussion of the purposes of the Establishment Clause, and for the fact that all nine justices agreed that the clause was intended to do far more than merely prohibit the establishment of a state religion.

Subsequent decisions make clear that a majority of justices on the Supreme Court view "the wall" separating church and state more as a shifting, porous barrier. Small factual differences in cases often produce different outcomes. For example, in 1948, the Court found that the practice of inviting religious instructors into public schools to give optional religious instruction violates the Establishment Clause. Then, in the 1952 case of *Zorach v Clauson*, the Court upheld the practice of giving public school students "release time" so that they could attend religious programs in churches and synagogues. Writing for the Court in Zorach, Justice Douglas said the Constitution does not require "callous indifference to religion."

The question of school-sponsored prayer has, of course, proven highly controversial. In the landmark case of *Engel v Vitale* in 1962, the Court ruled that New York's practice of beginning school days with a prayer drafted by school officials violated the Establishment Clause. This is the case, the Court said, whether or not students are given the option of not participating in the prayer. Following *Engel*, the Court has faced a whole series of prayer-related cases in the public school context raising issues such a prayer in special circumstances (e.g., graduation ceremonies), periods for silent meditation *or silent prayer*, and student-initiated prayer. In general, the Court has demonstrated a willingness to strike down any practices that might be likely to be perceived either as coercive or as a state endorsement of religion.[67]

This was truly the beginning of the end of religion in our society as we once knew it.

Robert Byrd, Senator from West Virginia (1917–2010)

Senator Byrd was elected the Democrat senator from West Virginia in 1959 and served until his death on June 28, 2010. He was a very controversial senator to say the least. He upset people, both conservatives and liberals. The one thing he was celebrated for was his knowledge and love for the Constitution of the United States. He always carried a copy of the Constitution in his coat pocket. Whenever a constitutional issue came up that he did not agree with, he would always pull out his copy and go right to the passage that was in dispute. He was probably one of the most patriotic of all senators or congressmen alike. He was proud of our country and defended its principles up until he died. In spite of his early reputation of being a segregationist, Senator Byrd was also a religious man.

Senator Byrd delivered a message on June 27, 1962, just two days after the U. S. Supreme Court declared prayer in schools unconstitutional, (*Engel v Vitale)*, warning Congress about disastrous decision such as this one:

> Inasmuch as our greatest leaders have shown no doubt about God's proper place in the American birthright, can we, in our day, dare to do less? ...In no other place in the United States are there so many, and such varied official evidences of deep and abiding faith in God on the part of government as here in Washington...Every session of the House and the Senate begins with prayer. Each house has its own chaplain.
>
> The Eighty-third Congress set aside a small room in the Capitol, just off the rotunda, for the private prayer and meditation of members of Congress... The room's focal point is a stained glass window showing George Washington kneeling in prayer. Behind him is etched these words from Psalm 16:1: **"Preserve me, O God, for in Thee do I put my trust."**

Inside the rotunda is a picture of the Pilgrims... Very clearly are the words, 'The New Testament according to our Lord and Saviour, Jesus Christ.' On the sail is the motto of the Pilgrims. ***"In God We Trust, God With Us."***

The phrase "In God We Trust," appears opposite the president of the Senate, who is the vice-president of the United States. The same phrase, in large words inscribed in the marble, backdrops the Speaker of the House of Representatives.

Above the head of the Chief Justice of the Supreme Court are the Ten Commandments, with the great American eagle protecting them...The crier who opens each session closes with the words, **"God save the United States and this Honorable Court."**

On the south banks of Washington's Tidal Basin, Thomas Jefferson still speaks:

God who gave us life gave us liberty. Can the liberties of a nation be secure when we have removed a conviction that these liberties are the gift of God? Indeed I tremble for my country when I reflect that God is just, that his justice cannot sleep forever.

Jefferson's words are a forceful and explicit warning that to remove God from this country will destroy it.[68]

And the LORD God of their fathers sent to them by his messengers, rising up betimes, and sending (warned); because he had compassion on his people, and on his dwelling place:
–2 Chronicles 36:15 (KJV)

Robert Byrd was right. By eliminating prayer in schools and by not teaching the Word of God, our country has been sliding down the path to oblivion. Every generation that has been deprived the Blessing of our Lord because it is "unconstitutional" to pray in school or to teach the Word of God, has seen a decline in moral values and traditional family values. As each generation falls farther away from the principles and guidelines of our Founding Fathers, as so eloquently written in our Constitution and other founding documents, our country falls farther away from the protection and promises of God our Father.

The decline in family values in our once great nation can be seen in every day life where the rights of parents are superseded by the "rights" of their children. Schools and other government bodies have taken away the fundamental rights and responsibilities God ordained to the parents. One example of this decline is that many children no longer respect the authority of their parents. They have gone so far as to challenging their parents in a court of law to get their own "rights" established. This is a direct contradiction of the Holy Scriptures.

For God commanded, saying, Honour thy father and mother: and, He that curseth father or mother, let him die the death.

–Matthew 15:4 (KJV)

COURT CASES AGAINST A CHRISTIAN NATION

U. S. Supreme Court case: AGUILAR v. FELTON, 473 U.S. 402 (1985)

New York City uses federal funds received under the Title I program of the Elementary and Secondary Education Act of 1965 to pay the salaries of public school employees who teach in parochial schools in the city. That program authorized federal financial assistance to local educational institutions to meet the needs of educationally deprived children from low-income families.

The Supreme Court ruled it "unconstitutional": *The Title I program administered by New York City, which is similar in a number of respects to that held unconstitutional today in School District of Grand Rapids v. Ball, ante, p. 373, violates the Establishment Clause.*

In his majority opinion, Justice Brennan wrote that this program differed from those at issue in *Grand Rapids School District v. Ball* (which were mostly permitted) because the classes were closely monitored for religious content. This "pervasive monitoring" did not save the program, however, because, by requiring close cooperation and day-to-day contact between public and secular authorities, the monitoring "infringes precisely those Establishment Clause values at the root of the prohibition of excessive entanglement."

Although it was true that the state's assistance to parochial schools did not have the ***primary*** effect of advancing religion, the close interaction between state and church nevertheless had that result. In short, the religious school, which has as a primary purpose the advancement and preservation of a particular religion, must endure the ongoing presence of state personnel whose primary purpose is to monitor teachers and students in an attempt ***to guard against the infiltration of religious thought.***

God forbid that our children should have religious thought! Just as the false teachers and false prophets in the time of Christ, there is an effort to blind the people to the truth of God. This is being done in the name of the U. S.

Constitution. This is a distortion of the truth of our Founding Fathers and the truth of our Lord Jesus Christ.

> *But there were false prophets also among the people, even as there shall be false teachers among you, who privily shall bring in damnable heresies, even denying the Lord that bought them, and bring upon themselves swift destruction.*
>
> **–2 Peter 2:1 (KJV)**

Graham v. Central Community School District of Decatur County
Civ. No. 85-335-B. States District Court, S.D. Iowa, C.D. May 9, 1985.
"This is a civil rights action under 42 U.S.C. § 1983, challenging the constitutionality of including an invocation and benediction at high school graduation ceremonies conducted by the defendant (Central Community School District). Plaintiff (Graham) seeks a declaratory judgment that including an invocation and benediction at the ceremonies violates the Establishment Clause of the First Amendment to the United States Constitution, which applies to the states through the Fourteenth Amendment, and they seek preliminary and permanent injunctive relief. Jurisdiction is predicated upon 28 U.S.C. § 1343(3)."

Finding:

> Religious invocation…in high school commencement exercises conveyed the message that district had given its endorsement to prayer and religion, so that the school district was properly prohibited from including invocation in commencement.

In other words it is "unconstitutional" to have prayers, benedictions, or religious invocations of any kind at a high school function. This is in direct contradiction to the intentions of our Founding Fathers, and those who followed them.

When our country was first founded most people could not read. The early settlers recognized the need to learn the Gospel and were dependent on traveling preachers to hear the Word of God. They realized that their survival was dependant on following God's Commandments and the teachings of Jesus Christ.

As the country began to grow the need for more preachers grew. The settlers began to learn to read and to teach the children to read for the sole purpose of *reading the Bible for themselves*. Public schools were established for this very reason.

Our Founding Fathers saw that the illiteracy of the country as a determent to having a stable society and a strong nation. They also saw the need to follow the Scriptures in our personal lives and the administration of the government.

As the nation grew in size the people begin to realize they needed to know more about what was going on around them. They began to teach in public schools things that would help them grow with the country. *This included the teaching of the Bible*.

The more people learned about our true history and about the Bible, the more prosperous our country became. This continued throughout our history until the twentieth century.

The Twentieth Century became a time to expand our horizons both at home and abroad. The more we learned, the more we prospered. We prospered and grew as long as we were faithful to Word of God. As long as we followed the Teaching of Christ, we were on the path of righteousness for the Glory of God. The Bible teaches us that all nations that follow the Will of God will grow in His Righteousness and Glory. But if you turn your back on Him you will lose favor with Him and turn to the path of oblivion and lose any hope of attaining a place in Heaven.

Ronald Reagan had said, we are "… the shining city on the hill…" This was true at one time, but now our nation is in a downward spiral and will hit bottom if we do not turn our attention back to God instead of the idol of power and the god of money. We must continue to teach from the Bible and to start to educate our current generation in the values of a moral and godly life.

From the time of our founding until 1980 all public buildings, i.e. courthouses, schools, libraries, etc. were allowed to display the Ten Commandments as a symbol of the laws that our country were founded on. It was not deemed to be forwarding any religious intent or belief. It was only a reminder that the laws of our country were drawn from the Laws of God, the Ten Commandments. Even the Supreme Court of the United States of America building has a very prominent display of the Ten Commandments.

To the right are pictures of the Ten Commandments on display in the Supreme Court Building in Washington D.C.

As you walk up the steps to the building which houses the U.S. Supreme Court you can see near the top of the building, a row of the world's law givers. Each one is facing the one in the middle who is facing forward with a full frontal view...*it is Moses and he is holding the Ten Commandments!*

As you enter the Supreme Court courtroom, the two huge oak doors have the *Ten Commandments* engraved on each lower portion of each door. It is the Law of Moses. As you sit inside the courtroom, you can see the wall, right above where the Supreme Court judges sit a display of the *Ten Commandments!*

Reward for keeping the Law of Moses

That thou mightest fear the LORD thy God, to keep all his statutes and his commandments, which I command thee, thou, and thy son, and thy son's son, all the days of thy life; and that thy days may be prolonged.3 Hear therefore, O Israel, and observe to do it; that it may be well with thee, and that ye may increase mightily, as the LORD God of thy fathers hath promised thee, in the land that floweth with milk and honey.

–Deuteronomy 6:2-3 (KJV)

Moses with the Ten Commandments in the rotunda of the Library of Congress

Moses told us to teach children.

And thou shalt teach them diligently unto thy children, and shalt talk of them when thou sittest in thine house, and when thou walkest by the way, and when thou liest down, and when thou risest up.

–Deuteronomy 6:7 (KJV)

Requirement to display Law of Moses in our homes.

And thou shalt write them upon the posts of thy house, and on thy gates.

–Deuteronomy 6:9 (KJV)

Moses also taught us:

But if ye will not hearken unto me, and will not do all these commandments;
15And if ye shall despise my statutes, or if your soul abhor my judgments,
so that ye will not do all my commandments, but that ye break my
covenant: 16I also will do this unto you; I will even appoint over you
terror, consumption, and the burning ague, that shall consume the eyes,
and cause sorrow of heart: and ye shall sow your seed in vain, for your
enemies shall eat it.

—Leviticus 26:14-16 (KJV)

Supreme Court decisions on the Ten Commandments
Stone v. Graham, 449 U.S. 39 No. 80-321
Decided November 17, 1980

Background Information
In Kentucky, the legislature passed a law requiring the posting of the Ten Commandments in each public school classroom in the state. The posters were paid for by private contributions and not state funds.

Perhaps expecting Establishment Clause challenges, the law also required the following notation at the bottom of each poster:

"The secular application of the Ten Commandments is clearly seen in its adoption as the fundamental legal code of Western civilization and the Common Law of the United States."

Court Decision
In a 5-4 Court Decision with a rare unsigned opinion, the Supreme Court ruled the Kentucky law unconstitutional.

The Court used the Lemon test (the test to determine if a law violates the First Amendment) to analyze the constitutionality of the Kentucky law, finding that it violated the first point—it did not have a secular legislative purpose.

The assertion by Kentucky at the bottom of the posters that its law had a secular purpose (to show students the influence of the Ten Commandments on the legal structure of Western society) did not necessarily make it so:

The pre-eminent purpose for posting the Ten Commandments on schoolroom walls is plainly religious in nature. The Ten Commandments is undeniably a sacred text in the Jewish and Christian faiths, and no legislative recitation of a supposedly secular purpose can blind us to that fact.

The posting of the Ten Commandments essentially lacks any valid educational function and the Court found it irrelevant that the copies were purchased with private contributions because the mere posting of the Commandments demonstrated official support of their message.

Significance

This decision stated that any requirement of religious symbols or teachings is sufficient to show governmental endorsement of their message, regardless of who ultimately funds them. Even if the schools hope for the Ten Commandments to be viewed through a secular framework, their historical and religious basis makes them irrefutably religious. This, then, makes such displays unconstitutional because the government is not permitted to endorse—directly or indirectly—any religious message or doctrine.

They that forsake the law praise the wicked: but such as keep the law contend with them.

–Proverbs 28:4 (KJV)

The following a from a commentary by Don Costello 7/20/2008 (Bible Studies)[69]

a. "Ten Commandments Thrown Out Of School", Cincinnati Enquirer, 11/18/80, Washington: "Thou shalt not post the Ten Commandments in public school classrooms, the Supreme Court told states Monday. By a 5-4 vote, the justices invalidated a 1978 Kentucky law requiring that a 16 x 20 inch copy of the Ten Commandments, purchased at private expense, be placed on the wall of every public classroom in the state. "The preeminent purpose for posting the Ten Commandments on school room walls is plainly religious in nature," the court majority concluded in an unsigned opinion issued without waiting for oral arguments and complete legal briefs. The state had argued that the statute did not violate the constitutional principle of church-state separation because no public funds were involved. Moreover, the state contended, the Ten Commandments brought down from Mt. Sinai by Moses in the Old Testament have become the foundation of American law. Those arguments were summarily rejected by the Court, which itself sits in a courtroom that includes Moses among its lawgivers. Above the justices' heads, in fact, is a marble panel depicting the Ten Commandments, flanked by the Majesty of the Law and the Power of Government."

b. Stone v. Graham was decided in 1980. It is the first Supreme Court case that dealt with the Ten Commandments and the second time it dealt with the Word of God in public schools. The posting of the Ten Commandments in public schools were declared unconstitutional because, the majority said, it failed the first prong of the Lemon test-a secular purpose.

c. Again I am reminded of the relationship of secular and profane. Paul warned Timothy [2 Timothy 2:16] that profane babbling will increase unto more ungodliness. This ruling was indeed a profane babbling and it increased unto more ungodliness.

   1). In Adams County, Ohio, this ruling was used as authority to force the county to remove the monument of the Commandments away from the school.
   2). It was used in Cobb County Georgia to force them to move its Ten Commandment plaque out of the courthouse.
   3). And lastly it was appealed to when McCreary County Kentucky and all U.S. County Courthouses were forced to remove the Ten Commandments from inside the courthouse.

d. In Stone v. Graham the majority wrote: "If the posted copies of the Ten Commandments are to have any effect at all, it will be to induce the school children to read, meditate upon, perhaps to venerate and obey, the Commandments. However desirable this might be as a matter of private devotion, it is not a permissible state objective under the Establishment Clause."

   1). I am reminded of Hosea 4:6 that says, "because thou hast rejected knowledge, I will also reject thee, seeing thou hast forgotten the law of thy God, I will also forget thy children." I am also reminded of Proverbs 1:30, 31 that declares that those who will have nothing to do with God's counsel or reproof shall eat the fruit of their own way and be filled with their own devices.

2). It was Martin Luther who wrote: "I am much afraid that schools will prove to be great gates of hell unless they diligently labor in explaining the Holy Scriptures, engraving them in the hearts of youth. I advise no one to place his child where the Scriptures do not reign paramount. Every institution in which men are not increasingly occupied with the word of God must become corrupt."

f. When elements of Stone v. Graham are compared with Miller v. California it will be revealed that the Supreme Court is more lenient toward pornography than it is toward the Commandments. In Miller v. California, a 1972 obscenity case, the Justices defined obscenity in three parts. The first, "whether the average parson, applying contemporary community standards, would find the work, taken as a whole, appeals to the prurient interest" The second part deals with state laws and doesn't concern us here. The third part is, "whether the work taken as a whole lacks serious literary, artistic, political or scientific value" The phrase used twice in this definition, "the work taken as a whole" is the leniency shown toward pornography. [This is the constitutional principle that became precedent in Roth v. U.S. See above.] In any pornographic publication, all that the publishers have to do is throw in a few articles on sports, biographies, or short stories and Presto! It's protected free speech because the whole work is considered.

1). But when it comes to the Ten Commandments, no such leniency is shown. In Stone v. Graham, the majority wrote, "The pre-eminent purpose for posting the Ten Commandments on schoolroom walls is plainly religious in nature. The Ten Commandments are undeniably a sacred text in the Jewish and Christian faiths, and no legislative recitation of a supposed secular purpose can blind us to that fact. The Commandments do not confine themselves to arguably secular matters, such as honoring one's parents, killing or murder, adultery, stealing, false witness, and covetousness. See Exodus 20:12-17; Deuteronomy 5:16-21. Rather, the first part of the Commandments concerns the religious duties of believers; worshipping the Lord God alone, avoiding idolatry, not using the Lord's name in vain, and observing the Sabbath Day. See Exodus 20:1-11; Deuteronomy 5:6-15.

2). Pornographic magazines are protected because, the publication must, "be taken as a whole." But the Ten Commandments are not allowed because, "they do not confine themselves to arguably secular matters", but also, "concerns the religious duties of believers." This is such a twisted interpretation; its only source of inspiration could be wicked spirits whispering into the ears of judges.

g. Stone v. Graham makes it unconstitutional to post the Ten Commandments at public schools or Courthouses. Yet two prominent Founding Fathers didn't believe incorporating at least two of the Ten Commandments into law were unconstitutional.

1). Oliver Ellsworth, On a Religious Test for Holding Public Office. "If any test were to be made, perhaps the least exceptionable would be one requiring all persons appointed to office to declare, at the time of their admission, their belief in the being of God, and in the divine authority of the Scriptures. In favor of such a test, it may be said that one who believes these great truths will not be so likely to violate his obligations to his country as one who disbelieves them; we may have greater confidence in his integrity. But I answer: His making a declaration of such a belief is no security at all. For suppose him to be an unprincipled man who believes neither the Word nor the being of God, and to be governed merely by selfish motives, how easy is it for him to dissemble! …But while I assert the rights of religious liberty, I would not deny that the civil power has a right, in some cases to interfere in matters of religion. It has a right to prohibit and punish gross immoralities and impieties; because the open practice of these is of evil example and detriment. For this reason, I heartily approve of our laws against drunkenness, profane swearing, blasphemy, and professed atheism."

* First printed in the Connecticut Courant and the American Mercury. Reprinted in The Annals of America, Vol. 3, 1784-1796, pp. 169-172, Published by Britannica.

* Oliver Ellsworth was a Connecticut delegate to the Constitutional Convention of 1787 and third Chief Justice of the Supreme Court, nominated by George Washington.

2). McGowan v. State of Maryland, 1961 Supreme Court case that upheld Sunday closing laws. Chief Justice Earl Warren authored the decision. "This Court has considered the happenings surrounding the Virginia General Assembly's enactment of "An Act for Establishing Religious Freedom", 12 Hening's Statutes of Virginia 84, written by Thomas Jefferson and sponsored by James Madison, as best reflecting the long and intensive struggle for religious freedom in America, as particularly relevant in search for the First Amendment's meaning. See the opinions in Everson v. Board of Education (US) supra. In 1776, nine years before the bill's passage, Madison co-authored Virginia's Declaration of Rights which provided, inter alia, that "all men are equally entitled to the free exercise of religion, according to the dictates of conscience" 9 Hening's Statutes of Virginia 109, 11-112. Virginia had had Sunday legislation since early in the seventeenth century; in 1776, the laws penalizing "maintaining any opinions in matters of religion, forbearing to repair to church, or the exercising any mode of worship whatsoever" (emphasis added), were repealed, and all dissenters were freed from the taxes levied for the support of the established church. Id., at 164. The Sunday labor prohibitions remained; apparently, they were not believed to be inconsistent with the newly enacted Declaration of Rights. Madison sought also to have the Declaration expressly condemn the existing Virginia establishment. This hope was finally realized when "A Bill for Establishing Religious Freedom" was passed in 1785. In this same year 1785, Madison presented to Virginia legislators "A Bill for Punishing Sabbath breakers" which provided, in part: "If any person on Sunday shall himself be found laboring at his own or any other trade or calling, or shall employ his apprentices, servants or slaves in labour, or other business, except it be in the ordinary household offices of daily necessity, or other work of necessity or charity, he shall forfeit the sum of ten shillings for every such offence, deeming every apprentice, servant, or slave so employed, and every day he shall be so employed as constituting a distinct offence." This became law the following year and remained during the time that Madison fought for the First Amendment in the Congress. It was the law in Virginia, and similar laws were in force in other States, when Madison stated at the Virginia ratification convention: "Happily for the states, they enjoy the utmost freedom of religion. Fortunately for this commonwealth, a majority of the people are decidedly against any exclusive establishment. I believe it to be so in the other states. I can appeal to my uniform conduct on this subject, that I have warmly supported religious freedom."

* In this quote from a Supreme Court case in 1961 we see that James Madison, in a nine year period from 1776 to 1785, not only successfully fought for religious freedom in Virginia and against the Established Church in Virginia; he also was successful in legislating elements of the Fourth Commandment in Virginia.

City Of Elkhart *v.* William A. Books
No. 00—1407. May 29, 2001

Background
William A. Books and Michael Suetkamp objected to a monument on the lawn of the City of Elkhart's Municipal Building inscribed with the Ten Commandments. The monument was erected in 1958 through a donation by the Fraternal Order of Eagles and through the efforts of judge E.J. Ruegemer who was concerned that failing to adhere to the Ten Commandments was contributing to juvenile delinquency. At the dedication ceremony, it was stated that if Americans accepted the Ten Commandments, they would receive "redemption from today's strife and fear."

The monument also contained images of two small tablets with Hebrew script, two Stars of David, and two superimposed Greek letters, Chi and Rho, symbolizing Jesus Christ.

A district court ruled that the monument did not violate the Establishment Clause of the First Amendment, arguing that it had a secular purpose both in promoting morality in youths and in promoting the significance of the Ten Commandments. The court also ruled that the monument did not have the effect of promoting or endorsing religion in any fashion.

Court Decision
According to the court, it isn't possible to strip the Ten Commandments of their religious significance and treat them as a document of secular ethics. The Ten Commandments do contain secular topics like duty to one's parents, but they also include religious topics like worshipping God.

The court also noted that the monument started out with the statement "I am the Lord thy God" in large lettering at the top. The religious element is further enhanced by the Stars of David and the distinctively Christian Chi Rho symbol.

The fact that the monument was undeniably religious is not enough, however, to judge it unconstitutional. Instead, it must be judged in the context in which it is presented. If the context is clearly secular in nature and intent, then the monument might be permissible—but no such context existed for this monument. On the contrary, the record showed that the City was involved in emphasizing the religious purpose of the display:

> In accepting the monument, the City... aimed to provide a code of conduct for the citizens of Elkhart to follow. The code chosen, however, was a religious code that focuses not only on subjects that are the legitimate concern of civil authorities, but also subjects that are beyond the ken of any government and that address directly the relationship of the individual human being and God. That the purpose was to endorse, through governmental sponsorship, a code of religious values is further established by the program of speakers at the dedication of the monument: a Protestant minister, a Catholic priest, and a Jewish rabbi.
>
> Indeed, this monument impermissibly suggests that, in this community, there are "ins" and "outs." The monument contains the Stars of David and the symbol of Christ, representing respectively Judaism and Christianity, two of the religions no doubt particularly represented in the Elkhart community, but by no means the total of all those who depend on the City of Elkhart as their local government.

Outcome

The 7th Circuit Court of Appeals agreed with the plaintiffs that the Ten Commandments monument was a violation of the Constitution. The monument, one of many erected across the country with funding from the Fraternal Order of Eagles, had to be removed because the Supreme Court refused to accept an appeal.

This decision reinforced the idea that there is a fundamentally religious nature to the Ten Commandments which cannot be readily overcome by protestations of secular purposes. Governments that want to post the Ten Commandments have a difficult argument to make—it's possible for a display to be permissible, but courts will look closely at the arguments used.

The comments made by Justices Rehnquist, Scalia, and Thomas are also important. Four votes are needed for a case to be accepted by the Supreme Court and evidently there were only these three—and it seems clear that these three would have voted with the City of Elkhart, finding such monuments to be constitutional. A shift of just one vote on the Supreme Court would mean that the next such case which comes up may be heard and may go in the other direction.

> *Remove not the ancient landmark, which thy fathers have set.*
> **–Proverbs 22:28 (KJV)**

Glassroth v. Moore (2002): Judge Roy Moore & His Ten Commandments Monument

Background Information

Roy Moore has a long history in Alabama as an advocate for the Ten Commandments and being challenged over his display of the Ten Commandments in his courts. In 1995 the ACLU sued him over this display and his practice of holding prayers before trials, but the suit was dismissed on a technicality.

In 2000, he was elected to the Alabama Supreme Court, partly on his fame and popularity over the Ten Commandments issue. On August 1, 2001, Chief Justice Moore unveiled a 5,280-pound granite monument in the rotunda of the Alabama State Judicial Building, which houses the Alabama Supreme Court, the Court of Criminal Appeals, the Court of Civil Appeals, the state law library, and the Alabama Administrative Office of Courts. This was done without consultation with other justices and after everyone had left for the day. The monument was placed alone in the center of the rotunda and anyone entering the building has no choice but to immediately see it.

The top of the monument is carved as two tablets with rounded tops which are engraved with the Ten Commandments as excerpted from the Book of Exodus in the King James Bible. Secular quotations about God are also on the sides of the monument, but Roy Moore, who designed the monument, emphasized that they were placed on the side rather than the top because those statements come from men rather than God and, hence, cannot be placed on the same plane. The purpose of the monument, according to Moore, is to begin a "restoration of the moral foundation of law to our people and a return to the knowledge of God in our land."

Court Decision

On November 18, 2002, a U.S. District Court ruled against Roy Moore, finding that the Ten Commandments constituted a violation of the Establishment Clause of First Amendment—indeed, that the evidence of this was "overwhelming."

It was clear that the purpose of the monument was in no way, shape or form secular. Moore made that evident when, at the public unveiling, he stated that it was there to remind people that the moral foundation of American law came from the Judeo-Christian God. Moore also made this purpose clear in trial over the monument:

> The Chief Justice gave more structure to his understanding of the relationship of God and the state, and the role the monument was intended to play in conveying that message. He explained that the Judeo-Christian God reigned over both the church and the state in this country, and that both owed allegiance to that God. ...The Chief Justice also explained at trial how his design and placement of the monument reflected this understanding of the relationship of God and the state. His design concerns were religious rather than secular in that the quotations were placed on the sides of the monument instead of on its top because, in keeping with his religious belief, these statements were the words of man and thus could not be placed on the same plane with the Word of God. Similarly, he rejected the addition, along side the Ten Commandments monument, of a monument containing Rev. Dr. Martin Luther King, Jr.'s "I Have a Dream" speech, not for secular reasons but because the speech was not "the revealed law of God."

There is no question that Moore's purpose was religious. He wanted to tell everyone entering the Alabama State Judicial Building—including the judges, lawyers, and other public employees who work there—that the god Moore believes in is sovereign over them and over the laws which Moore interprets when rendering his decisions.

That this monument was intended to depict the Ten Commandments as a sacred document was made evident when the judge visited them:

> The court was captivated by not just the solemn ambience of the rotunda (as is often true with judicial buildings), but by something much more

sublime; there was the sense of being in the presence of something not just valued and revered (such as an historical document) but also holy and sacred.

This makes Moore's Ten Commandments display dramatically different from displays in other public contexts. Other displays try to emphasize secular aspects of the Ten Commandments, for example their role in the development of law and legal codes in Western civilization. Moore was utterly opposed to such a display because he regarded the Ten Commandments in purely religious terms.

Judge Thompson further found that the monument was a violation of the principle that government action must not have the primary effect of either advancing or inhibiting religion. It is not simply that a "reasonable observer" aware of Moore's history and beliefs will understand that the monument is designed to endorse particular religious views, but the monument even violates the "coercion test" proposed by some of the harshest critics of the endorsement test, like Supreme Court Justices Kennedy, Rehnquist and Scalia:

> [The monument] is nothing less than "an obtrusive year-round religious display" installed in the Alabama State Judicial Building in order to "place the government's weight behind an obvious effort to proselytize on behalf of a particular religion," the Chief Justice's religion.

Significance

Roy Moore is a celebrity for the Christian Right in America. Moore's perpetual court cases over his various Ten Commandments displays were a popular cause for fundamentalists around the country. Because of this, the decision has played an important role in the relationship not only between church and state, but also between separationists and America's religious right.

Alabama's judicial ethics panel removed Chief Justice Roy Moore from office in November 2003 for defying a federal judge's order to move a Ten Commandments monument from the state Supreme Court building.

What role can the Ten Commandments play in American law and American politics? People want to display the Commandments to encourage people to either remain or become faithful to Judeo-Christian traditions and Judeo-Christian religious beliefs. How overt can the religious proselytization be in fundamentalists' efforts to remake America in their own image of a godly society? Display of the Ten

Commandments can be justified by a secular context, but here that justification was abandoned in favor of an explicit religious tone.

McCreary County, Ky. V. ACLU of Kentucky (docket #: 03-1693) (2005)

Background

McCreary County, Kentucky, put up a Ten Commandments display in the county court house. After it was challenged, the county added several more documents referencing religion and God: the Congressional Record from 2/2/83 proclaiming a Year of the Bible, an excerpt from the Declaration of Independence stating "all men… are endowed by their Creator with certain unalienable rights," a quote from the Constitution of Kentucky stating "We, the people from the Commonwealth of Kentucky, grateful to Almighty God"; President Lincoln's proclamation of a Day of Prayer, President Reagan's proclamation that 1983 was the Year of the Bible, a copy of the Mayflower Compact invoking the "name of God," and a picture of Abraham Lincoln with a quote from him saying "The Bible is the best gift God has ever given to man."

In 2000, this display was declared unconstitutional. The court noted that the County selected only documents or portions of documents expressing favoritism towards certain religious ideas; therefore, it could not be claimed as an effort to educate people about legal or cultural traditions in America. In some cases, the editing of the documents arguably distorted their original context and meaning in order to endorse a religious meaning preferred by the county.

Rather than appeal, the county changed the display to include the Ten Commandments alongside the full text of the Magna Carta, the Declaration of Independence, the Bill of Rights, the Star Spangled Banner, the Mayflower Compact of 1620, a picture of Lady Justice, the National Motto, and the emblem and preamble to the Kentucky Constitution. Each document was accompanied by explanations of their significance. With the Ten Commandments, the display said that they constituted the "moral" background of America's legal traditions.

ACLU Arguments

According to the ACLU, it might be legitimate to display the Ten Commandments if some explanation of their connection to American law or government is made, but the McCreary County display didn't do this—it merely asserted that the Ten

Commandment are the moral background of the law. The McCreary County display was not a secular message and the various documents did not "share a common secular theme or subject matter." Thus, the purpose of the display was religious rather than secular.

It must also be remembered that the Ten Commandments continue to be an active symbol of religion and an active expression of particular religious dogmas. They are not merely historical by any stretch of the imagination. This means that special care must be taken in any display of the Ten Commandments, even in a display that is arguably constitutional, but McCreary County didn't do this. On the contrary, the history of the display reveals that they had the promotion of religion in mind all the time. They argue that they want to educate people about the law, but that is mere pretense.

Finally, it is clear that the effect, as well as the purpose of the law, is to promote religion. No connection between the Ten Commandments and any of the other documents is explained; it's asserted, but that's not the same thing. A reasonable observer would therefore not see any connection, and would interpret the display of the Ten Commandments as an effort to promote them as such, rather than as anything connected to the origins of American law.

McCreary County Arguments

According to McCreary County lawyers, the Ten Commandments are displayed in court houses all over the nation, making the display in McCreary County unremarkable. They are simply a facet of America's heritage as a Christian Nation and shouldn't arouse any great opposition, even from non-Christians. We don't object to displays of documents like the Declaration of Independence which reference God, so why should we object to the Ten Commandments simply because they reference God?

Lawyers acknowledged that the original Ten Commandments display was deeply flawed, reflecting not only religious intent but also producing a religious effect. They argued, though, that they had seen the error of their ways during the first court challenge and that is why they drastically altered the display currently being challenged. This new display removed all the problematic religious references and the county shouldn't be punished further for doing the right thing.

Moreover, when arguing before the Supreme Court lawyers for the County claimed that any inquiry into the purpose behind such displays was misguided because true "purpose" is unknowable—thus, trying to make such an inquiry is merely and invitation for judges to impose their own assumptions upon the actions of others. This was a curious argument given the fact that inquiries about the purpose of a law are a standard aspect of so many legal judgments.

Outcome

The Supreme Court upheld the Sixth Circuit Court decision that even under the amended display, there was no integration of the Ten Commandments with secular material such that the entire display could be said to have a "secular message." The nature of the original display made it clear that the whole purpose was to send a "religious message" and that the changes were made merely to get around constitutional limitations.

In his majority opinion, Justice Souter emphasized the principle that government must remain neutral between various religions as well as between religion and no religion:

> The display's unstinting focus was on religious passages, showing that the Counties were posting the Commandments precisely because of their sectarian content. That demonstration of the government's objective was enhanced by serial religious references and the accompanying resolution's claim about the embodiment of ethics in Christ. Together, the display and resolution presented an indisputable, and undisputed, showing of an impermissible purpose.

In her concurring opinion, Justice O'Connor emphasized the fact that the government doesn't have the authority to promote religious beliefs merely because they are followed by a majority:

> It is true that many Americans find the Commandments in accord with their personal beliefs. But we do not count heads before enforcing the First Amendment. ...Nor can we accept the theory that Americans who do not accept the Commandments' validity are outside the First Amendment's protections. There is no list of approved and disapproved beliefs appended to the First Amendment...

These Court rulings, disavowing our Christian heritage, is leading us away from what our Founding Fathers intended, **_One Nation Under God._** As a direct result of these actions our children and there children will not be afforded the Constitutional right of religious freedom. The freedom of religious expression is one of our strongest and heartfelt rights afforded to us by the Constitution of the United States.

Our Founding Fathers and all of the leaders following in their path risked their lives, property and honor to achieve this one basic right. Thousands upon thousands of our military, both men and women, have given their lives to defend this right and the right to live in freedom. Freedom to worship when and how they chose. Freedom to live in a nation not controlled by a tyrannical government. They died during the Revolutionary War, the war of 1812, the Civil War, World War I, World War II, Korea, Viet Nam, Iraq, and Afghanistan and other parts of the world. These brave patriots died so that we may live in a free society. A society founded on Judeo-Christian beliefs.

Our courts and our government are slowly eroding the very essence of a free society.

Ah sinful nation, a people laden with iniquity, a seed of evildoers, children that are corrupters: they have forsaken the LORD, they have provoked the Holy One of Israel unto anger, they are gone away backward.
–Isaiah 1:4 (KJV)

Not only has our nation been damaged by the Supreme Courts rulings in the past 50 years, but also be rewriting history, (omitting facts of our history). The following excerpt from David Barton's "American's Godly Heritage" (1993), shows how our children were once instructed how our country was influenced by God and by the teaching of Jesus Christ; it also showed how one person was protected by God's grace.

Before the American Revolution our country was in another war. The American French and Indian War (1753–1763).

A well-documented (but today unfamiliar) part of America's Godly heritage involves the account of young George Washington during a fierce military battle in which his life precariously hung in the balance for two hours but was miraculously spared. In fact following that event, Washington himself openly acknowledged that it had been by the direct intervention of God that he remained alive...July 9, 1755, General Edward Braddock, commanding the American forces, headed toward a French fort...over the next two hours, 714 of the 1.300 British and American troops were shot down, …even among the officers the British losses had been enormous: of the eighty-six British and American officers in that battle, 26 were killed and 36 more were wounded. Significantly, George Washington was the **only** mounted officer not shot down off his horse—and he had been particularly vulnerable, having courageously ridden back and forth along the front lines, delivering General Braddock's orders among the troops.

Late in the battle General Braddock was seriously wounded and George Washington took charge, gathering the remaining troop and headed back toward Fort Cumberland.

Along the way Braddock died, and upon his death, Washington performed the role of a military chaplain, conducting the funeral service, reading Scriptures, and offering prayers…During the week-long return to the fort, word had spread across the colonies that the slaughter of the British and Americans had been complete—that the entire force had been wiped out. After his safe arrival at the fort, Washington wrote a letter to his family, assuring them that despite reports to the contrary, he was still very much alive.

Having confirmed his safety to his family, he then recounted what had occurred during the battle—that when he removed this jacket at the end of the battle, he found four bullet holes through it but not a single bullet had touched him; he had horses shot from under him, but he had not been scratched. He therefore concluded:

> I now exist and appear in the land of the living by the miraculous care of Providence that protected me beyond all human expectation.

As word of God's Divine protection of Washington spread across the colonies, the Rev. Samuel Davies referred to the incident in a sermon only a few weeks after the momentous battle:

> …As a remarkable instance of this, I may point out to the public that heroic youth Col. Washington, whom I cannot but hope Providence has hitherto preserved in so signal (remarkable) a manner for some important service to his country.

Davies' expectant hope for the young Washington proved to be quite accurate. Twenty years later, it was apparent that God definitely had selected Washington for and "important service to his country," and the entire nation has benefited as a result. In fact, nearly two centuries later President Calvin Coolidge confirmed:

> He (Washington) was the directing spirit without which there would have been no independence, no Union, no Constitution, and no Republic... We cannot yet estimate him. We can only indicate our reverence for him and thank Divine Providence which kept him to serve and inspire his fellow man.

Significantly, Washington himself recognized that the critical role he had played in America's formation was not the result of his own skills but rather the favor of God. As he openly acknowledged, 'I have only been an instrument in the hands of Providence.'

Additional evidence of just how miraculous had been Washington's preservation in 1755 was provided fifteen years later in 1770 when Washington had occasion to return to the same Pennsylvania woods where he had earlier battled the French and Indians. An old Indian chief, hearing that Washington had come back to the area, traveled to meet with him. The ancient leather-faced chief sat down with him over a council fire and announced that he had been a leader in the battle against Washington fifteen years earlier.

The chief recounted that during the battle, he had instructed his braves to single out the officers and shoot them down, knowing that if they could slaughter the officers, they could scatter the remaining troops and then easily destroy them later. Like the other officers, Washington had been specifically singled out. In fact, the chief proudly explained that his rifle had never before been known to miss, but after having personally fired at Washington seventeen different times without effect, he concluded Washington was under the care of the Great Spirit and therefore instructed his braves to stop firing at him. He then told Washington:

> I have traveled a long and weary path that I might see the young warrior of the great battle. I am come to pay homage to the man who is the particular favorite of Heaven, and who can never die in battle.

> *The LORD will preserve him, and keep him alive; and he shall be blessed upon the earth: and thou wilt not deliver him unto the will of his enemies.*
> **–Psalms 41:2 (KJV)**

This remarkable account of God's direct intervention in the life of one of our national heroes appeared in American history textbooks for nearly a century and a half; it is a well-documented part of our Godly heritage but is an account virtually unknown today. In fact, now we are regularly told just the opposite— that America had no Godly heritage and that four Founding Fathers were atheists, agnostics, and deists who formed a completely secular government. However, a clear pronouncement by Founding Father John Adams proves otherwise. Adams forcefully declared:

The general principles of which the fathers achieved independence were…the general principles of Christianity.[70]

And the LORD shall make thee the head, and not the tail; and thou shalt be above only, and thou shalt not be beneath; if that thou hearken unto the commandments of the LORD thy God, which I command thee this day, to observe and to do them:

–Deuteronomy 28:13 (KJV)

Chapter Five

OUTLAWING RELIGIOUS EDUCATION IN CHRISTIAN NATION

The fear of the LORD is the beginning of knowledge...
–Proverbs 1:7 (KJV)

Our Founding Fathers and many of our past leaders certainly understood this truth, and from the beginning of the founding of our nation, until recent history, stressed the relationship between a sound education based upon biblical truths and the future of the nation.

President Theodore Roosevelt said: "To educate a person in mind and not in morals is to educate a menace to society..."

In Supreme Court decisions rendered in 1962 and 1963, which struck down religious activities, such as school prayer and Bible reading, in major activities of daily student life in public schools redefined the way the our children are being taught. The courts determined that to have a prayer at school functions, such as sporting events and graduation ceremonies was "unconstitutional". It was the first time in the history of the United States that any branch of the federal government took such a stand, censoring religious activities long considered an integral part of education.

This sudden restructuring of educational policies was precipitated by the Court's controversial reinterpretation of the phrase "separation of church and state" as it relates to the First Amendment. This simply states, **"Congress shall make no law respecting and establishment of religion or prohibit the free exercise thereof."** The Court decided that the First Amendment includes a prohibition against including religious activities in public affairs, inviting skyrocketing numbers of lawsuits that challenge any presence of religion in public life. The Court has already delivered far-reaching decisions to:

- Remove Student prayer—*Engle v. Vitale,* 1962
- Remove school Bible readings—*Abington v. Schempp,* 1963
- Remove the Ten Commandments from view—*Stone v. Graham,* 1980
- Remove benedictions and invocations from school activities—*Graham v. Central,* 1985; *Kay v. Douglas,* 1986; *Jager v. Douglas,* 1989; *Lee v. Weisman,* 1992.

Remove not the ancient landmark, which thy fathers have set.
–Proverbs 22:28 (KJV)

The actions of the U. S. Supreme Court have been in direct contradiction to what the Founding Fathers intended. Prior to 1962 the high court has always ruled in favor of the religious intent of the Founders. Now with the liberal leaning of the courts in the 1960's we have eliminated one of the key strengths of our nation, the belief and faith in Almighty God.

When prayer was removed from our schools in 1963 in another attempt to rid America of any reference to God, President Ronald Reagan recognized the danger of this act when he said:

Our Pledge of Allegiance state that we are 'one nation under God,' and our currency bears the motto, 'In God We Trust.' The morality and values such faith implies are deeply embedded in our national character. Our country embraces those principles by design, and we abandon them at our peril. Yet in recent year...Americans...have for the sake of religious tolerance forbidden religious practices in the classrooms. The law of the land effectively removed prayer fro our classrooms. How can we hope to retain our freedom through the generations if we fail to teach our young that our liberty springs from an abiding faith in our Creator?[71]

Another step in our moral decline was made as America's citizens began to accept the beliefs of others as equal truths. Toleration lead to the reclassification of homosexuality as a mental illness in 1973. Now it is promoted in public education through "celebration of diversity" curriculum. Laws against sodomy were forced out of state legislation by the ACLU. Sex before marriage became acceptable through implementing standards of "Common Law Marriage" and the convenience of abortion. While Americans cry out against weapons of mass destruction, abortion claims millions of lives. Dullness of heart compounds the dullness of mind. As with each generation, the new citizens of America became more unable to live by the words of the apostle Peter:

But sanctify the Lord God in your hearts: and be ready always to give an answer to every man that asketh you a reason of the hope that is in you with meekness and fear:
                                                                     –1 Peter 3:15 (KJV)

Always be ready to give a defense to everyone who asks you a reason for the hope that is in you. How can they defend hope which they no longer have?

It is interesting to note that early Americans were facing a land of emptiness; their future and all their well-being held no security. Therefore, these people recognized their daily need for God, and their circumstances kept them dependent on Him. However, as America has grown to be a world leader and is economically stable, our society has forsaken God, not recognizing their constant need for Him.

The words of Jesus ring so true:

And again I say unto you, It is easier for a camel to go through the eye of a needle, than for a rich man to enter into the kingdom of God.
                                                                     –Matthew 19:24 (KJV)

Scripture makes it quite clear what must be done to reverse the tide of evil, yet many Christians wonder why America is in such a dire situation, while at the same time disregarding God's admonition:

If my people, which are called by my name, shall humble themselves, and pray, and seek my face, and turn from their wicked ways; then will I hear from heaven, and will forgive their sin, and will heal their land.

–2 Chronicles 7:14 (KJV)

The following is from **The Importance And Method Of Teaching Children Morality** by Philip Atkinson[72]

How A Civilization Keeps Itself Alive
Civilization is a shared understanding, and the only way a civilization can maintain this understanding from generation to generation is by that understanding being passed from parent to child, which is how a civilization keeps itself alive.

Importance Of Early Infantile Experience
The nature of an understanding depends upon its founding values, which makes morality (the actual values adopted) the vital concern for parents, with the early experiences of infancy the most critical for the formation of understanding in a child. This means that the lessons taught to the infant during the first weeks or months of its existence are the most important, as every subsequent value must reflect those values already adopted by the maturing mind of the person. For once the foundation of values is set; it is for life, with the values taught during child rearing becoming a permanent part of the adult's understanding.

Morality Must Be Imbued By Fear Of Authority
As reason can only be employed when morality is established, teaching children morality must be by the clear demonstration of right from wrong by the unquestioned implementation of parental discipline: the swift punishment of naughty children—a correction that must be feared to be effective.

Unquestioning Obedience Of Authority An Essential Lesson
Even after the age of seven years of age, when the child can reason, instruction must be continued without explanation, as unquestioning obedience to authority is one of the requirements of a dutiful citizen.

Continuation Of Tradition

The basic values and knowledge that are the foundation of Tradition—those beliefs that are implicit in the customs, manners, language, and laws of the community—must be taught in the same unexplained way; not just to reinforce the notion of the need for unquestioning obedience, but also because these beliefs are an essential part of communal understanding and so *must* be adopted by all citizens. Observe, these beliefs were created by the genius of communal understanding, which is superior to each citizen's comprehension, so disqualifying any individual from being able to properly judge the reasons behind such beliefs. Hence it is not just the child's duty to adopt these beliefs without question, but it is the parent's duty to impose them without explanation.

Consequences Of Failure

If parents fail to teach their offspring the basic morality and knowledge that are the foundation of the tradition of the community, then the resulting adult will fail to become a useful citizen, but will become a problem citizen—an individual with an understanding different and incompatible to the shared understanding that is the community. Once such problem citizens become sufficient in numbers then the community must decay until it finally dissolves.

Mr. Atkinson is stating to how and why morals are important in a civilized society. It is the duty of the parents to teach morality to their children, not the state. From the time of our founding, parents have taken this responsibility seriously. Now the state through the public school system is trying to dictate to the parents that morals are not important.

Secular Humanism

The main emphasis on teaching morals today (or lack thereof) comes from the people and leaders of this nation that believe in Secular Humanism. What is Secular Humanism?

Secular Humanism is an attempt to function as a civilized society with the exclusion of God and His moral principles. During the last several decades, Humanists have been very successful in propagating their beliefs. Their primary approach is to target the youth through the public school system. Humanist Charles F. Potter writes, "Education is thus a most powerful ally of humanism, and every American school is a school of humanism. What can a theistic Sunday school's meeting for an hour once a week and teaching only a fraction of the children do to stem the tide of the five-day program of humanistic teaching?" (Charles F. Potter, "Humanism: A New Religion," 1930)[73]

Theologically, Secular Humanists are *atheists*. Humanist Paul Kurtz, publisher of Prometheus Books and editor of *Free Inquiry* magazine, says that "Humanism cannot in any fair sense of the word apply to one who still believes in God as the source and creator of the universe." Corliss Lamont agrees, saying that "Humanism contends that instead of the gods creating the cosmos, the cosmos, in the individualized form of human beings giving rein to their imagination, created the gods."[74]

Philosophically, Secular Humanists are *naturalists*. That is, they believe that nature is all that exists —the material world is all that exists. There is no God, no spiritual dimension, no afterlife.[75]

Atheism leads most Secular Humanists to adopt *ethical relativism*—the belief that no absolute moral code exists, and therefore man must adjust his ethical standards in each situation according to his own judgment. If God does not exist, then He cannot establish an absolute moral code.[76]

The only way to achieve the goal of these Secular Humanists is to remove God from the class room. They have done this in many ways, mostly through the courts.

We have had prayer removed from the class room, we have had religious documents and sayings removed from schools and public buildings. The Pledge of Allegiance is being challenged constantly because of the words "Under God" is in it.

Any mention of God or Christianity is forbidden in public forums and exercises. Why then does the U.S. Senate and House of Representatives open each session with a prayer? Our money says "In God We Trust". The Supreme Court building is full of the Ten Commandments and other religious sayings and prayers.

Children are being suspended from school for expressing the religious beliefs in an attempt to exercise their Constitutional right of religious expression. Parents are being taken out of the equation in the education of their children.

The Corruption of our Children

In an effort to teach morals to our children we are thwarted by the state in public schools that teach sex education instead of sexual abstinence. The state run schools teach that homosexual relationships are alright for an alternative lifestyle, even though the parents might disagree.

In 1997 in Northboro, Massachusetts parents demanded that a high school teacher be fired for teaching about sexuality and possible homosexual experiences.

He gave his students (in history mind you) a list of sixteen questions relating to sexuality. Among them were:

> What do you think caused your heterosexuality? Is it possible your heterosexuality is just a phase which you might outgrow? Considering the menace of overpopulation, how would the human race survive if everyone was heterosexual like you? How can you become a whole person if you limit yourself to compulsive, exclusive heterosexuality? Should you at least try to develop your natural, healthy, homosexual potential? [77]

This is just one example of how our schools are moving from teaching basic moral values, to teaching that it's alright to have sex out of wedlock and to any other alternative lifestyle contrary to the Bible. They stress "safe sex" instead of "no sex". We as a nation must take over the control of our children's lives and the education of traditional family values.

In a 1994 column, Phyllis Schlafly gave some of the history on sex education and the results.

> Sex education started coming into public schools about 30 years ago, and became progressively more explicit until many courses include actual demonstrations of how to use contraceptives and pornographic videos to explain the facts of life to minor children...often without the knowledge of the parents.[78]

In 1997 California state Assemblywoman Sheila Kuehl introduced AB101, a bill to widely broaden rights on the basis of "sexual orientation". The bill would require school districts to use textbooks which place gay lifestyle on the same moral level as a heterosexual family, prevent campus religious groups from refusing membership to practicing homosexuals, and deny use of school facilities to groups which oppose homosexuality like churches, the Boy Scouts, etc. Fortunately for our children, AB101 failed on a vote of 36-40. That is much too close!

School-based clinics and sex-ed programs schools in many states became a major source for distributing condoms to students, often without parental knowledge or permission. Opponents of the condom program said abstinence is the primary message that should be conveyed—and having the schools distribute condoms doesn't reinforce that message.

Television is another area that is used to "re-educate" our society. It seems one can hardly watch TV anymore without being bombarded with profanity, sexually explicit content, or scantily clad women prancing around—and that just the commercials. Today's "sit-coms" promote sexual promiscuity, profanity, homosexual relationships while ridiculing the traditional family values. The dramas are even worse. They not only promote the same things as the "sit-coms", but they include violence in every imaginable area of life including, abortion, rape, etc.

When I was growing up in the '50's watching TV was a form of entertainment that actually **promoted** family values. If there was a bedroom scene it was always with a married couple, fully clothed (usually in pajamas) lying in separate twin beds. Teenagers were never shown in sexually compromising situations as in today's programs. Even the dramas were promoting family values. You never saw a star that played a good guy in one program play a bad guy in another program. It sounds silly now but in the movies and TV the good guys always wore the white hat.

One of my favorites was Roy Rogers and Dale Evans. For many of us who grew up with them, they always felt so much more personal than other Hollywood royalty. In their fanciful movie and TV dramas they took their position as stars to heart and always tried to set a good example. They cared about the influence they had on all the little "pardners" in their thrall, and they weren't embarrassed to tell us so. Dale often liked to tell her own children as well as the rest of us, "Your life is the only Bible some people will ever read"; and for us youngsters who adored them, Roy and Dale truly were an inspiration of near-biblical significance. If our own parents weren't around to help or maybe sometimes didn't provide such good examples, the King of the Cowboys and the Queen of the West were there to show us how to live: how to make a slingshot from the prongs of a vining maple tree, how to shoot straight and ride smooth, how to be brave at times when we were scared, how to be decent human beings in the face of bushwhackers and bad guys.

The bad guys always lost and the good guys always won, not matter what. In programs it was not unusual to refer to a family going to church. They even showed them going to church, can you imagine? That's when they actually had "censors" in Hollywood that would review everything that went on television and in the movies. If it was "dirty" or profane, it would not be allowed. Some say well what about freedom of speech? Keep in mind not all speech is protected under the First Amendment. You can't yell "fire" in a crowed room and be protected. To some sexual content and profanity is the same as yelling fire. Hate speech is not protected either. The perversion of our youth is to some, Hate Speech.

When I was going to school in the 50's and 60's things were much different then than they are today. During elementary school and junior high school we would start out each day saying the Pledge of Allegiance to the flag. Yes we said "and one nation **Under God.**" We also had a time to pray if we chose to. Yes these were public schools. When I reached high school we could no longer say the Pledge of Allegiance or say a prayer. These two freedoms were taken away by the liberals of this country, by saying that the words "Under God" and any form of prayer, was outlawed because it was "unconstitutional."

Times were simpler then, I admit. However the degree that our society has declined in its moral values and judgment is frightening.

Through the re-education of our children in the public school system and the perversion on television, our future is one of darkness and despair. With the government prohibiting the worship of God in public and the display of Christian symbols being banned in community areas, the only road we are on is the road to Hell.

Only through the Word of God can we help to reverse this trend. We must as believers make every effort to combat the powers in our government and our schools with the Truth of the Bible and the teaching of Jesus Christ.

It is because of the liberal agenda that people in power have towards society, that we have become a second rate nation. We have lost the moral high ground that we once so proudly proclaimed. We have lost our moral compass that generations upon generations proclaimed in the name of our Lord Jesus Christ.

The Attack on Christianity

The following is an excerpt from "The White House Attack on Religion Continues" (06/03/09) by David Barton, founder of Wallbuilders (with permission)

Some of the first acts of the new presidential administration make it clear that there has been a dramatic change in the way that traditional religious faith is going to be handled at the White House. For example, when the new White House website went public immediately following the inauguration, it dropped the previously prominent section on the faith-based office.

A second visible change was related to hiring protections for faith-based activities and organizations. On February 5, President Obama announced that he would no longer extend the same unqualified level of hiring protections observed by the previous administration but instead would extend those traditional religious protections to faith-based organizations only on a "case-by-case" basis.

Significantly, hiring protections allow religious organizations to hire those employees who hold the same religious convictions as the organization. As a result, groups such as Catholic Relief Services can hire just Catholics; and the same is true with Protestant, Jewish, and other religious groups. With hiring protections, religious groups cannot be forced to hire those who disagree with their beliefs and values—for example, Evangelical organizations cannot be required to hire homosexuals, pro-life groups don't have to hire pro-choice advocates, etc.

Hiring protections are inherent within the First Amendment's guarantee for religious liberty and right of association, and were additionally statutorily established in Title VII of the 1964 Civil Rights Act. Congress subsequently strengthened those protections, declaring that any "religious corporation, association, education institution, or society" could consider the applicants' religious faith during the hiring process. The Supreme Court upheld hiring protections in 1987, and Congress has included those protections in numerous federal laws. But when Democrats regained Congress in 2007, on a party-line vote they began removing hiring protections for faith-based organizations.

The current concern about the weakening of traditional faith-based hiring protections is heightened by the White House's announcement of President Obama's commitment to "pass the Employment Non-Discrimination Act, to prohibit discrimination based on sexual orientation." This act would fully repeal faith-based hiring protections related to Biblical standards of morality and behavior, thus directly attacking the theological autonomy of churches, synagogues, and every other type of religious organization by not allowing them to choose whether or not they want to hire homosexuals onto their ministry staffs.

The administration's third attack on religion occurred in the President's stimulus bill, which included a provision specifically denying stimulus funds to renovate higher educational facilities "(1) used for sectarian instruction or religious worship; or (2) in which a substantial portion of the functions of the facilities are subsumed in a religious mission." As Republican Senator Jim DeMint (SC) explained, "any university or college that takes any of the money in this bill to renovate an auditorium, a dorm, or student center could not hold a National Prayer Breakfast." Sen. DeMint therefore introduced an amendment to "allow the free exercise of religion at institutions of higher education that receive funding," but his amendment was defeated along a party-line vote.

The fourth attack on tradition religious faith appeared in President Obama's 2010 proposed budget, which included a seven-percent cut in the deduction for charitable giving. Experts calculate that this will result in a drop of $6 billion in contributions to charitable organizations, including religious groups.

The fifth attack is the White House's announcement that it will seek the repeal of conscience protection for health care workers who refuse to participate in abortions or other health activities that violate their consciences. [79]

We as a nation have allowed this to happen. Because of the decline of moral values in this country and the political apathy that prevails in our society, we allowed one of the most ardent enemies of Christianity to be elected to the presidency and allowed his liberal companions in Congress to chip away at our Constitutional rights of freedom of religion.

We as a nation can turn this around. We must as Christians and patriots take a stand against this kind of evil. We must pray to our Lord God for forgiveness of our personal sins and also the sins of our nation. We can no longer sit by and hope that someone else will to it. Only we as believers can do it! **WE MUST ACT <u>NOW</u>!**

Chapter Six

TAKING BACK OUR
CHRISTIAN NATION

W ith the educational system currently in place in America, ignoring and omitting the basic tenants of Christianity to teach our children the Word of God we are in direct violation of God's commandments:

And thou shalt teach them ordinances and laws, and shalt shew them the way wherein they must walk, and the work that they must do.
                                                                                      –Exodus 18:20 (KJV)

...but teach them thy sons, and thy sons' sons;
                                                                                      –Deuteronomy 4:9 (KJV)

Now these are the commandments, the statutes, and the judgments, which the LORD your God commanded to teach you, that ye might do them in the land whither ye go to possess it:
                                                                                      –Deuteronomy 6:1 (KJV)

In a recent survey of America's knowledge of religion, it was found atheists (yes this is a religion), agnostics, Jews and Mormons knew more about their religion than Catholics and Christians. This is a frightening declaration. It is the duty of all Christians to reach out and teach the Word of God to non-believers. How can we teach if we don't know the basic tenents of our own belief?

It is because of the lack of teaching the Christian philosophy in our schools over the last 50 years that has led us to this alarming place in our history. Only by turning back to God can we hope to gain the glory that God once bestowed on us. If we continue on this course of self-destruction we will surely see the wrath of God. Just as Israel turned their back on God and was punished, so shall we be punished? The Lord is quite clear about that.

> *The LORD shall send upon thee cursing, vexation, and rebuke, in all that thou settest thine hand unto for to do, until thou be destroyed, and until thou perish quickly; because of the wickedness of thy doings, whereby thou hast forsaken me.*
>
> **–Deuteronomy 28:20 (KJV)**

Pray for America

As Christians, it is our responsibility to pray for America. Not just in time of national crisis, but always. With due respect for the Supreme Court, the Congress, and the president, they are not the source of our future or our hope. Only God and the power of the Holy Spirit can sustain the strength and future of this nation.

> *...The effectual fervent prayer of a righteous man availeth much.*
>
> **–James 5:16 (KJV)**

Throughout the Bible we see how prayers moved the hand of God and changes came to nations, leaders, laws, and individuals.

First, as God's people, we must humble ourselves and confess to God the sins of our nation as well as our own lives—our self-centeredness, lusts, addictions, the love of the world, and any area in which we are disobeying His Word. God has said:

If my people, which are called by my name, shall humble themselves, and pray, and seek my face, and turn from their wicked ways; then will I hear from heaven, and will forgive their sin, and will heal their land.

–2 Chronicles 7:14 (KJV)

Second, we must pray for our leaders and authorities. Ask the Lord to give godly wisdom, protection, and direction to the president, Congress, state and local officials, judges, and others who God had raised up to lead His people. The Bible says:

That they may offer sacrifices of sweet savours unto the God of heaven, and pray for the life of the king, and of his sons.

–Ezra 6:10 (KJV)

1 Let every soul be subject unto the higher powers. For there is no power but of God: the powers that be are ordained of God. 2 Whosoever therefore resisteth the power, resisteth the ordinance of God: and they that resist shall receive to themselves damnation. 3 For rulers are not a terror to good works, but to the evil. Wilt thou then not be afraid of the power? do that which is good, and thou shalt have praise of the same: 4 For he is the minister of God to thee for good. But if thou do that which is evil, be afraid; for he beareth not the sword in vain: for he is the minister of God, a revenger to execute wrath upon him that doeth evil. 5 Wherefore ye must needs be subject, not only for wrath, but also for conscience sake.

–Romans 13:1-5 (KJV)

If we see nonbelievers taking control of the government, passing laws that violate the laws of God, and jeopardizing our God-given freedoms, our mandate is to intervene and trust God to restore godliness to our nation and communities. We can only do this at the ballot box. We must look for godly people and elect them to lead us. We, as Christians, have the moral obligation to try to defeat any ungodly person running for office, no matter what the cost or consequence.

But the eyes of the wicked shall fail, and they shall not escape, and their hope shall be as the giving up of the ghost.

–Job 11:20 (KJV)

Third, we must pray that the Lord will work in a powerful way in the hearts of Christians and people from all walks of life.

Come, and let us return unto the LORD: for he hath torn, and he will heal us; he hath smitten, and he will bind us up.

–Hosea 6:1 (KJV)

Only God has the power to free people from the sins that destroy their lives as well as the foundations of righteousness. Only God has the power to save our nation.

Fourth, we must pray for families, for schools systems, for the military, for the economy, and for the vital aspects of our society. Be aware of what is going on, and pray. Only God can save us through His Glory and Mercy.

[1] I exhort therefore, that, first of all, supplications, prayers, intercessions, and giving of thanks, be made for all men; 2 For kings, and for all that are in authority; that we may lead a quiet and peaceable life in all godliness and honesty.

–1 Timothy 2:1-2 (KJV)

Prepare for Battle

The survival of our nation is dependent on the Grace of God. We must as Christians be prepared to battle all evil influences in our government and in our society in general. The existence of the power of Satan is evident in all aspects of our lives. We have let it grow. As a cancer grows in our body, the evil in our culture grows unabated. Just as we would seek medical treatment for our body, we must seek spiritual treatment for our nation. We can only achieve this through prayer and repentance. We must be prepared to combat the forces of the ungodly influences in our lives and ask God for the wisdom and courage to go forward in our spiritual warfare with Satan and his minions.

Be of good courage, and he shall strengthen your heart, all ye that hope in the LORD.

–Psalms 31:24 (KJV)

Jonathan Mayhew (1720–1766)

Jonathan Mayhew was a Congregational minister and lecturer at Harvard in 1765, reflected on the colonists' feelings toward King George III's hated Stamp Act:

The king is a much bound by his oath not to infringe the legal rights of the people, as the people are bound to yield subjection to him. From whence it follows that as soon as the prince sets himself above the law, he loses the king in the tyrant. He does, to all intents and purposes, un-king himself.

But now thy kingdom shall not continue: the LORD hath sought him a man after his own heart, and the LORD hath commanded him to be captain over his people, because thou hast not kept that which the LORD commanded thee.

–1 Samuel 13:14 (KJV)

Mayhew also noted that while people are generally willing to accept the leadership of there nation if it is *fair* and *just*, they will **revolt** when **abused** and **oppressed**.

Till people find themselves greatly abused and oppressed by their governors, they are not apt to complain; and whenever they do, in fact, find themselves thus abused and oppressed, they must be stupid not to complain

This is exactly where our country is today. We have a government that has usurped the powers of the people for their own end. Because our nation as a whole has turned their back on God in every area of life, He has allowed the sacred rights given to us by Him to be taken away by our government. Our government is no longer headed by a Godly leader, but by an ungodly tyrant.

We **MUST** as a nation, take back our country from this tyrannical government and bring it back to the Glory of God as it was first founded over 250 years ago.

> *The wicked walk on every side, when the vilest men are exalted.*
> **–Psalms 12:8 (KJV)**

The United States Has Had a Glorious Status Because of God [80]

We, the United States of America, have been the greatest society, nation, and people that has ever existed in history. Through our people and their innovations, the United States has brought comfort and convenience to the world. Because and through American Generosity, the destitute, poor, wretched, and even entire nations have benefited wonderfully. The sole reason for this international influence is because for the first one hundred and eighty years of our history, the United States of America gave God his rightful place. In recent times, the US has declined, most glaringly in our military presence and economic strength. However, if we as a society will hearken back to the reason for our explosive growth, massive expansion, and towering influence, we can and will, again, have such power and strength as we have ever known. As the Bible declares time and time again, we, as a society, must repent and turn back to God in whole hearted faith. The United States had been great because the people of the United States had been good, and we had been good because we had kept our focus on God.

Just as God blessed Israel for obeying His law and worshipping Him, so shall the Lord bless the United States of America if we return to Him.

> *And it shall come to pass, if thou shalt hearken diligently unto the voice of the LORD thy God, to observe and to do all his commandments which I command thee this day, that the LORD thy God will set thee on high above all nations of the earth:*
> **–Deuteronomy 28:1 (KJV)**

> *And all people of the earth shall see that thou art called by the name of the LORD; and they shall be afraid of thee.*
> **–Deuteronomy 28:10 (KJV)**

And I will bless them that bless thee, and curse him that curseth thee: and in thee shall all families of the earth be blessed.

–Genesis 12:3 (KJV)

Even in the face of mounting problems, massive economic trials, military challenges, and un-Godly initiatives, we as a society can still repent and turn back to God. If we will, collectively and individually, return to God, he will return to us. His word promises in 2nd Chronicles that if his people will call on his name, he will turn and save us. God has blessed the USA. If we want to continue to experience his blessings, we must return to him. It's not too late.

We are at a cross roads for our nation. We can either continue on the path to destruction or turn back to God and ask Him to forgive us and bless us once again. We were once a proud Godly nation that cared about our neighbors and were willing to help them no matter what it hardship it would create. This was a matter of personal choice, not a mandated action created by an ungodly government. The path we are currently on is one that will doom us to oblivion. The moral fiber of this once great nation has deteriorated to the point that God may not be willing to over look it much longer. Just as in Sodom and Gomorrah the Lord saw an abomination unto his eyes and destroyed the people who were wicked in there thoughts and actions, so he will do to us if we do not repent and ask for forgiveness and his eternal blessings.

We do not know when our Lord will come to pass judgment on all the earth and all who live here. We only know that it will happen. Unless we seek God's forgiveness we will be doomed to eternal damnation. We cannot "wait to see what happens" in hopes of gaining favor at the last minute. No favor will be given, no blessings will be given, no eternal life with the Lord will be given if we "wait and see". We must bring our nation back from the brink of the abyss. We must take action now in order to save our country from oblivion. Most of us are Born Again Christians and now we must become born again Americans. We must make every effort to bring our country back to God.

We must, as Americans, go back to the words of Thomas Jefferson:

The way to have good and safe government is not to trust it all to one, but to divide it among the many, distributing to everyone exactly the functions in which he is competent ...

- To let the National Government be entrusted with the defense of the nation, and its foreign and federal relations …
- The State Governments with the Civil Rights, Laws, Police and administration of what concerns the State generally.
- The Counties with the local concerns, and each ward direct the interests within itself.

It is by dividing and subdividing these Republics from the great national one down through all its subordinations until it ends in the administration of everyman's farm by himself, by placing under everyone what his own eye may superintend, that all will be done for the best.

We must, as Americans, go back to the words of Abraham Lincoln in his Gettysburg Address:

…that this nation, under God, shall have a new birth of freedom — and that government of the people, by the people, for the people, shall not perish from the earth.

Let us, as Americans, consider the words of Samuel Adams:

…The necessity of the times, more than ever, calls for our utmost circumspection, deliberation, fortitude and perseverance. Let us remember that, "if we suffer tamely a lawless attack upon our liberty, we encourage it, and involve others in our doom," it is a very serious consideration … that millions yet unborn may be the miserable sharers of the event.

We, as Americans, should never live in fear of our government. However, look around you. Every where we are there the government is, using its might and power to block some of our more basic rights. The government has grown so powerful that every aspect of our lives are controlled by it. This is by no means what the founding fathers intended.

We, as Americans, should heed these words of Thomas Jefferson:

When the government fears the people there is liberty; when the people fear the government there is tyranny.

To reemphasize the words of Jonathan Mayhew, quoted previously:

Till people find themselves greatly abused and oppressed by their governors, they are not apt to complain; and whenever they do, in fact, find themselves thus abused and oppressed, they must be stupid not to complain

We must complain. Complain at the ballot box. It is the duty of each American citizen to vote. It is our sacred duty ordained by God to vote for our elected officials and insure we get a government that believes in the Word of God and the teachings of Jesus Christ.

Noah Webster stated:

God commands you to choose for rulers, just men who will rule in the fear of God. The preservation of a republican government depends on the faithful discharge of this duty; if the citizens neglect their duty and place unprincipled men in office, the government will soon be corrupted; laws will be made, not for public good, so much as for selfish or local purposes; corrupt or incompetent men will be appointed to execute the laws; the public revenues will be squandered on unworthy men; and the rights of the citizens will be violated or disregarded.[81]

Now therefore behold the king whom ye have chosen, and whom ye have desired! and, behold, the LORD hath set a king over you.
–1 Samuel 12:13 (KJV)

The words of Noah Webster, written over 200 years ago, ring true today. We have elected "unprincipled men" to office in all areas of our government. Our government has been corrupted and laws have been made, "not for public good, so much as for selfish or local purposes." "Corrupt or incompetent men" have been appointed to execute the laws, and "the public revenues" have been "squandered on unworthy men" and "the right of the citizens" have "been violated or disregarded."

The laws, people, and money Mr. Webster warned us about have come to reality. Our basic right of freedom of religion has been denied us by these same men.

For we wrestle not against flesh and blood, but against principalities, against powers, against the rulers of the darkness of this world, against spiritual wickedness in high places.

–Ephesians 6:12 (KJV)

If we believe that the Founding Fathers were correct in asserting that America would fail if it lost its religious foundation, it is primarily incumbent upon Christian believers to reaffirm and reclaim our Christian educational heritage with the same passion and commitment of the Founders. There are many ways and many levels at which to instigate change, but it begins with a willingness to become engaged in battle.

We must engage in battle. We must battle the powers that control this once great nation with the power of God. We must turn back to our founding principles of Christianity and take back our government created by the people, for the people, as one nation under God.

We are on a slippery slope here and we must take the reigns and make sure we don't fall off the cliff into oblivion. God blessed this country once and let's all make sure he blesses us again. If we want to be the "nation under God", with the Christian principles and Christian ethics that was the foundation of this great country, we must act now. We must all pray for our country and pray for our leaders to once again seek the council and the wisdom from our Lord, Jesus Christ. We must contact all our friends and relatives, all our co-workers and ask everyone we meet to pray for our nation and to ask for deliverance from the evil that is so abundant in our society. We must be like Paul Revere and give the warning of impending doom if we do not seek the blessings of God.

Pray for our country and our leaders. Pray that our leaders get the wisdom to lead us back to the land of our Puritan founders. A One Nation Under God that is America. Pray to God for forgiveness of all of our sins, personal and national. We must beg forgiveness and truly repent our sins for God to hear our prayer. Pray that God forgive our nation for the sins of excess and sins of omission. Beg forgiveness for our nation's sins against its citizens and the sins against all mighty God.

All mighty father and merciful God, we pray that you give the Wisdom of Solomon and the patience of Job to our leaders so they might lead us back to the path of righteousness. Father forgive this nation for all of its sins against you and against the citizens of this once great nation. Heavenly Father bless this great nation of ours and help us to return to the teachings of our Lord Jesus. We pray that our leaders can see the path you set forth for this great nation 400 years ago. Let us not be like the ancient Israelites who turn their back on you after being delivered from Egypt. Let us see the error of our ways and come back to the loving and merciful God that you are.

Dear Lord let us be willing to be used by You to help turn this great nation back to your Glory. Let us stand up and make our lives to be the strength in our families and neighborhoods and workplaces. Let us all go forth and make an effort to bring our state and national leaders back into the righteousness that God had proclaimed to our Founding Fathers. We know You want to come and bless us, to forgive our sins and heal our nation. Please oh Lord, give us all the courage and strength to go forward and tell all who will listen, that we must bring our country back to the Lord our God, in Jesus name we pray.

Amen

And when He was come near, He beheld the city, and wept over it...."
– Luke 19:41 (KJV)

ENDNOTES

[1] http://edwards.yale.edu/research/about-edwards/biography

[2] http://www.ravenhill.org/edwards.htm

[3] http://www.christianitytoday.com/ch/1993/issue38/3802.html

[4] http://www.preaching.com/resources/past-masters/11548788/page-5/

[5] CliffsNotes.com. *Enlightenment and Religious Revival.* 28 May 2010

[6] The American Patriots' bible page 565 I - 17-18.

[7] http://www.crf-usa.org/bill-of-rights-in-action/bria-13-4-a.html

[8] http://www.articlemyriad.com/enlightenment_america.htm

[9] http://www.loc.gov/exhibits/religion/rel04.html Religion and the Founding of the American Republic.

[10] The American Patriot's Bible page 500 insert

[11] http://www.greatseal.com/committees/firstcomm/

[12] The American Patriot's Bible page 935

[13] http://www.wallbuilders.com/libissuesarticles.asp?id=90

[14] http://www.loc.gov/exhibits/religion/rel06-2.html

[15] The Faith of the Presidents, Ron DiCianni , page 14

[16] http://www.wallbuilders.com/LIBissuesArticles.asp?id=105 (James Madison)

[17] The American Patriot's Bible page 64

[18] The American Patriot's Bible page 720

[19] America's Godly Heritage, David Barton, page 8

[20] http://churchstatelaw.com/cases/WatsonvJones.asp

[21] http://www.wallbuilders.com/LIBissuesArticles.asp?id=105

[22] The American Patriot's Bible page 690

[23] http://www.wallbuilders.com/LIBissuesArticles.asp?id=58

[24] http://www.lucidcafe.com/library/95sep/adams.html

[25] http://www.acton.org/publications/randl/rl_liberal_en_368.php

[26] http://americasfoundingfathers.com/index.php/bookshelf

[27] The American Patriot's Bible page 829

[28] The American Patriots' Bible page 201

[29] http://lsm.crt.state.la.us/cabildo/cab4.htm

[30] http://www.america.gov/st/educ-english/2008/April/20080407113519eaif
     as0.3545038.html

[31] http://www.tlogical.net/biofinney.htm

[32] http://www.biblebelievers.com/Grady1.html

[33] The American Patriot's Bible page 1403

[34] The American Patriots' Bible page 182

[35] http://nationalhumanitiescenter.org/tserve/nineteen/nkeyinfo/cwnorth.htm

[36] The American Patriot's Bible page 371

[37] http://www.wallbuilders.com/libissuesarticles.asp?id=53

[38] The American Patriot's Bible page 1067

[39] The American Patriot's Bible page 448

[40] The American Patriot's Bible page 1303

[41] Vidal v Girard's Executor, 43, U.S. 126, 205-206 (1844)

[42] America's Godly Heritage; David Barton (1993) page 26

[43] People v Ruggles, 8 Johns 545, 547 (1811)

[44] America's Godly Heritage; David Barton (1993) page 30

[45] The American Patriot's Bible page 535

[46] http://www.adherents.com/people/ph/Rutherford_B_Hayes.html

[47] http://www.whitehouse.gov/about/presidents/theodoreroosevelt/

[48] [James Lever, *The Roosevelt Mythos* 1923. p 191]

[49] http://www.eadshome.com/TheodoreRoosevelt.htm

[50] http://www.adherents.com/people/pw/Woodrow_Wilson.html The American
     Patriots' Bible page 180 (insert)

[51] The American Patriots' Bible page 217

[52] Elizabeth Edwards Spalding, "True Believers" *Wilson Quarterly* 2006

[53] http://www.adherents.com/people/pt/Harry_S_Truman.html

[54] The American Patriots' Bible page 180 (insert)

[55] http://www.adherents.com/people/pe/Dwight_Eisenhower.html

[56] http://www.beliefnet.com/News/Politics/2004/02/Reagans-Penchant-For-Prayer.aspx?p=1

[57] http://www.positiveatheism.org/writ/ghwbush.htm

[58] http://www.adherents.com/people/pb/George_W_Bush.html

[59] http://www.baptiststandard.com/2003/2_17/pages/bush_preacher.html

[60] http://kclibrary.lonestar.edu/19thcentury1800.htm

[61] The American Patriot's Bible I-22 and I-23

[62] http://www.earlyamerica.com/review/winter96/jefferson.html

[63] The American Patriot's Bible page 820

[64] The American Patriot's Bible page 681

[65] http://www.archives.gov/exhibits/charters/constitution_founding_fathers_connecticut.html

[66] The American Patriot's Bible page 1295

[67] http://www.law.umkc.edu/faculty/projects/ftrials/conlaw/estabinto.htm Establishment Cls

[68] http://christianactionleague.org/news/senator-robert-byrd

[69] http://crossfaithministry.org/proverbs-284.html

[70] America's Godly Heritage; David Barton (1993) pgs 13-17

[71] http://www.hyperhistory.net/apwh/essays/cot/t4w32usmoraldecline.htm

[72] http://www.ourcivilisation.com/moral2/moral3.htm

[73] http://www.secular-humanism.com/

[74] http://www.christiananswers.net/q-sum/sum-r002.html

[75] None Dare Call It Education, by John A. Stormer (1998) page 21

[76] ibid; page 23

[77] http://www.wallbuilders.com/LIBprinterfriendly.asp?id=23592

[78] http://www.raptureready.com/soap/L48.html

[79] http://www.rightsidenews.com/200906035014/life-and-science/culture-wars/the-white-house-attack-on-religion-continuesrepealing-conscience-protection.html

[80] http://www.raptureready.com/soap/L48.html

[81] The American Patriot's Bible page 316

Printed in the USA
CPSIA information can be obtained
at www.ICGtesting.com
JSHW022336140824
68134JS00019B/1515